"Passing along his wide breadth of experience and talents to the next generation of leaders in *The Bet*, Jay Rodgers offers priceless, high-level guidance for achieving business success and helping entrepreneurs maximize their impact."

—GINO WICKMAN
Bestselling Author of *Traction: Get a Grip on Your Business* and *The EOS Life: How to Live Your Ideal Entrepreneurial Life*

THE BET

THE BET

An Entrepreneur's All-In Strategy to Win in Business

JAY D. RODGERS

BROWN BOOKS
PUBLISHING GROUP

© 2023 Jay D. Rodgers

The Bet
An Entrepreneur's All-In Strategy to Win in Business

Brown Books Publishing Group
Dallas, TX / New York, NY
www.BrownBooks.com
(972) 381-0009

A New Era in Publishing®

Publisher's Cataloging-In-Publication Data

Names: Rodgers, Jay D., author.
Title: The bet : an entrepreneur's all-in strategy to win in business / Jay D.
    Rodgers. Description: Dallas, TX ; New York, NY : Brown Books Publishing
    Group, [2023]
Identifiers: ISBN: 9781612546285 (hardcover) | LCCN: 2022950924
Subjects: LCSH: Rodgers, Jay D. | Businesspeople--United States--Biography. |
    Entrepreneurship—
Anecdotes. | Success in business--Anecdotes. | LCGFT: Autobiographies. |
    Anecdotes. | BISAC: BUSINESS & ECONOMICS / Entrepreneurship.
    | BIOGRAPHY & AUTOBIOGRAPHY / Business. | BUSINESS &
    ECONOMICS / Decision-Making & Problem Solving.
Classification: LCC: HC102.5.R554 A3 2023 | DDC: 338.092--dc23

ISBN 978-1-61254-628-5
LCCN 2022950924

Printed in Canada
10 9 8 7 6 5 4 3 2 1

For more information or to contact the author, please go to
www.JayRodgersAuthor.com.

My book is written for and dedicated to those seriously committed entrepreneurs who are growing companies, creating employment, and strengthening the foundation of our great country.

"As you travel the entrepreneurial road to success, remember there are two miles of ditch for each mile of road."

—Jay D. Rodgers

— Contents —

— Foreword —

Jay Rodgers is an original. No one who knows him would argue that fact. As an example, I want to share with you how the two of us met about a dozen years ago.

One day, on my private line, I got a call from a stranger with a booming voice and a Texas drawl—a man who proudly announced he'd been able to locate my unlisted number.

"I'm Jay Rodgers," he said. "From Texas." (By then, I *knew* he was from Texas.) He went on to say, "I wanted to hate you."

Then he explained that he had written a book and had a particular title, one he really wanted to use, in mind. As it turns out, the title, *Street Smarts*, had already been used by another entrepreneur-author—me.

"So I read your book, and it's so good that I forgive you for stealing my title," he said. "You do a lot of the same things I do. Mr. Brodsky, I want to take you to lunch."

"Well," I told him, "I'm in Manhattan, and you're in Texas. Where do you think we should meet?"

"Any place you say, any time you say, I'll be there."

I said, "Sure." I had to meet this guy. Anyone who had the guts to call me up like that was worth meeting.

I've never regretted accepting that invitation. We did have that lunch, and we struck up a friendship of many years. After I got to know Jay, I saw that he helps people and gives back in the same ways

I do. We share the same entrepreneurial spirit, the same love for business, and we both want to pass on the knowledge we've acquired over the years.

When you get to a modicum of success and you have a few things in this world, wouldn't you want to share what you know? Not everyone does. A great entrepreneur is not necessarily one who makes a zillion dollars; it's someone who sees things, creates things, and makes things better—someone who leaves an impact on people and the world. True entrepreneurship is a way of thinking. You start a business to make a living. After that, what else is there? I believe it is service, it is sharing. That's what I do and what Jay does.

Jay cares, and it shows in the work he does for his nonprofit, Biz Owners Ed. Most speakers are paid for public speaking. For Biz Owners Ed, however, those who are invited to be mentors pay their own expenses and make a $5,000 donation to Biz Owners Ed to speak there. Where else in the world would anyone do that? It's an example of the power of Jay Rodgers. During the pandemic, I started Whiskey Wednesday, a place for those of us with like minds to gather and talk about business. That group continues to grow, and many of Jay's associates join us.

As I said before, Jay Rodgers is an original. He is also one of the greatest entrepreneurs of our time. I invite you to share his wisdom in this book.

—**Norm Brodsky**
Coauthor of *Street Smarts* and *The Knack* and Entrepreneur in Residence at the Birthing of Giants Fellowship Program

— Publisher's Note —

The familiar patois of celebratory exchanges resonated across the marble tabletop, where Jay D. Rodgers had just set aside his unsigned publishing contract. An impromptu discussion on his untitled manuscript ensued.

At that point, Rodgers said, "There's just one last thing. If I'm going to sign this contract, you need to agree to a bet."

"What kind of bet?" I asked, stunned.

"I want to bet you $10,000 that the book will not sell out its first printing within a year."

With that, he earned the unprecedented distinction of rendering me speechless—though only momentarily.

Once I could assemble a request for clarification, I asked, "You mean you're betting against . . . yourself?"

"I am," he replied, casually.

Without further hesitation, I stuck out my hand to shake on it and said, "Yes!" Then I added, "My only concern is where and how to spend my winnings. And I can't wait!"

As it unfolded, our mutual, Texas-sized commitment to upending the status quo was confirmed, and he signed the contract.

"Oh, one last thing," I added. "Your book now has a title. We're going to call it *The Bet*."

⚜ ⚜ ⚜

The happy aftermath of our meeting affirmed I'd been right to believe, or at least to hope, I shared the unapologetically independent ethos I'd recognized when I first encountered Rodgers's brand of entrepreneurship.

Over the past two-plus decades, I've watched as his string of wildly successful endeavors took him from leader to legend. I've read up as the media devoured quips from the former cowboy as he played up his roots, once positing the art of raising pumpkins as a model for mergers and acquisitions. I have learned and absorbed as much as I can from various windows into Rodgers's perspective.

Erstwhile, I was working seven days a week (still do) to grow my business, and Rodgers and I would occasionally cross paths at CEO gatherings and other professional circles. Over time, I became acquainted with the man behind the larger-than-life persona, deepening my respect and appreciation for his unerring wisdom. And I certainly wasn't the only one who considered him a Lone Star State sage.

When Rodgers talks, billionaires, founders, friends, and students alike stop to listen. With an endless supply of witticisms and a particular style of Texas pride and bravado, his presence often evokes John Wayne—who is featured prominently in Rodgers's headquarters where a signed letter from the late great hangs in his office.

Long before I became his publisher, Rodgers had already come to represent my idea of the ideal author for Brown Books. After all, I built my company as the "Entrepreneurial Publisher for Entrepreneurial Authors."

Three decades later, our platform is both a reflection of and a vehicle to elevate the voices of distinct, all-around leaders like those I admire. In other words, individuals like Rodgers.

Shortly after I eagerly accepted Rodgers's wager, I discovered a comically apt phrase that crystallized exactly how I wound up involved in such an unorthodox gamble. Apparently, it's a common adage at the poker table, but not being much of a card shark myself, it was new to me.

"Play the man, not the cards" was the version I heard, though I'm told there are many variations on the phrase. The moment I digested that idiom, I knew I'd been played by Rodgers.

And I subsequently saw the sincere compliment hiding in the subtext of his offer. Rodgers—a man whose legacy I'd long admired and respected—had discerned me as his contemporary, since only a fellow entrepreneur who'd recognized something of himself in me could've known which bargain would be surefire bait.

He knew I'd take his bet. I have built up my brand as a publisher known for its excellence, and there is no way I cannot let him sell out his first print run—I never saw it as a problem in the first place.

Once we began developing his manuscript, I was further impressed—if not surprised—by the tangible authenticity of his wager. Betting big on yourself and others is among the key messages Rodgers imparts in the coming chapters, and in my rather extensive experience, an entrepreneur who literally embodies his own advice is both rare and *always* a reliable source for an interesting read.

Though it's beyond even my capabilities to fully convey Rodgers's inimitable character in the confines of the written word, and I've merely scratched the surface of his *joie de vivre* on these pages, you will more deeply understand his essence after reading his renegade business book—which is certainly not a paint-by-numbers approach. If you're unfamiliar with Rodgers, I'm honored you've chosen this book as your introduction to him and his work, and hope you'll feel as if you've met a new mentor. If you're already a friend or fan of the author, I hope you'll be able to hear his voice or picture his likely expression as you read each word.

Either way, if you enjoy *The Bet*, please tell all your friends, enemies, frenemies, family members, or anyone else within shouting distance to buy a first edition without delay—because I've already made big plans for my $10,000 win.

—**Milli Brown**
Founder and CEO of Brown Books Publishing Group

— Introduction —

Why I Made the Bet

When I'm in the process of negotiating a deal or transaction, I frequently start by asking myself the question: "What would be the very best outcome for each of the participants involved?" If there's more than one desired outcome for a participant, I list and prioritize those outcomes. I think I developed this approach over the years from

1. my belief that the best way to get what you want is to spend your time helping other people get what they want;

2. the old adage, "If you can see John Jones through John Jones's eyes, you can sell John Jones what John Jones buys;"

3. my belief that the best deals you'll ever make will be with smart people;

4. the best negotiations are win-win; and

5. smart people add value to any deal, making it easier to achieve the win-win outcome—meaning it is much better to lose 59 percent to 61 percent than to win 51 to 49 percent.

When I decided to write this book, I spoke to three of my friends who had worked with Brown Books Publishing Group and had been extremely pleased. Then I met with Brown's founder and owner—my old friend, Milli Brown. As always, I was impressed by Milli's pride in her company and the results they produced. And I was pleased to see that Milli was as competitive as ever. She told me that authors whose books like mine provide usable, meaningful value to the reader frequently receive royalties that offset all of the publishing charges.

I knew that entrepreneurs who are successful bet on themselves; sometimes that faith in your abilities and your belief in the outcome are all you have. I also knew that Milli had gotten where she is today by betting on Brown Books in its early days. So, as a condition for signing the contract, I presented her with a wager: I bet her $10,000 that my book *wouldn't* sell out its first printing. At first, she seemed stunned, and then her eyes lit up, and she put out her hand to shake on it. You see, the best deals are the ones where everybody wins.

The bet was simply my Entrepreneurial Strategic Thinking. I made the bet knowing that Milli was the only person who could lose—and that she would devote all of her considerable power to make sure I did. The success of this book is now tied to Brown Book Publishing Group's reputation and Milli's personal pride. Just weeks after I signed on, she flew a top professional photographer in from California to shoot the cover. God bless, Milli can now use my book to promote her publishing company, and she watched over the entire project like a pro. I, of course, burned the midnight oil thinking about how I could help her win our bet. That's called Entrepreneurial Strategic Thinking.

I hope this book inspires you to bet on your dreams, your hope, and yourself.

—1—

Entrepreneurial Mindset

Entrepreneurs are a lot like cowboys: if you're not a risk-taker, gun-slinger, or willing to dodge a few bullets or bulls, you may not be well suited to be an entrepreneur. Most successful entrepreneurs I know take calculated risks and think they're going to win. No one wants to take a risk where you think you'll lose, but occasionally you do experience a loss or you make a bad decision—and that's okay. It's all part of the journey.

Before I set out on the journey to formally become an entrepreneur, I worked for Kodak. I say "formally" because I was an entrepreneur from an early age, starting one business or another and always finding ways to make money. Many entrepreneurs who come to my table for advice started out that way. If you asked, they'd tell you they were always inquisitive as a child and ready to create a business, even if it was a roadside lemonade stand. Entrepreneurs share a few common traits, and you'll find me talking about them in this book:

1. **Entrepreneurs always ask**. They ask for the business, and sometimes they even ask for more than the other person wants to give.

2. **Entrepreneurs seize opportunity when they see it**. Make sure you're not at the movies when your ship comes in.

3. **Entrepreneurs always learn**. They tend to see every victory and even failures as a growth experience.

If you're an entrepreneur, it's inevitable that you'll eventually be the only one who believes in a decision you've got to make. That means you've got to go against the grain and take risks. Entrepreneurs are willing to take a risk and bet on themselves.

Four months after I transferred with Kodak from Rochester, New York, to Dallas, Texas, a man in a rumpled, white dress shirt came in the back door of the advertising department, walked into my office, and said, "I'm with Elko stores, and my name is Pat."

He told me he needed some window displays for several of their Dallas stores. At that time, we had beautiful, thirty-by-forty-inch color photograph enlargements that we gave stores to use in their displays. I took him to our storage area, and we picked out the photographs he wanted. I asked him how he got to the office. He had flown into nearby Dallas Love Field Airport and took a cab over. I offered to drive him to his downtown Dallas hotel, thinking that Elko's display man would appreciate saving a little money on his expense account.

We hit it off immediately, and on our way to the Adolphus Hotel where he was staying, I suggested that we go to lunch. He said that would be great, but he wanted to go by the hotel first to change shirts since his was rumpled from the flight.

When we got there and went straight to the President's Suite, I knew I had missed something. Turns out he was *the* owner of the Elko card and photo stores located throughout the Midwest and was one of our division's largest customers.

We went on to lunch, and we both really enjoyed getting acquainted. I told him about the thousand-line Christmas ad that Kodak was going to run in the *Dallas Morning News* and suggested that he take out a tie-in ad next to ours on the page. He didn't respond. I took him back to his hotel and went back to work.

The next day, I called the *Dallas Morning News* and asked them to do a mockup of the ad with an Elko tie-in ad that covered the remainder of the page. My partner at Kodak and the ad department at the *Dallas Morning News* were sure that Elko wouldn't agree to the tie-in because they had never done so in the past. However, they played along with me as the new guy and agreed to do the mockup. Four or five days later, they gave me a nice mockup in a presentation folder. The next day, my phone rang, and a man's voice asked, "How many offers have you had today for a free lunch?"

"Who is this?"

The man replied, "Why does it matter if it's free?" It was Pat.

After lunch, we went back to Pat's suite and had a few drinks. I showed him the mockup of the ad from the *Dallas Morning News*, and he didn't say yes, no, or "go fish." I tossed the ad across the room, and it fell behind the couch.

After a few more drinks, we decided to go out again. Pat suggested we go to an early dinner; I agreed, and he directed me to the Dallas Love Field Airport. There was a great restaurant on the second floor of the airport, and I assumed that's where we were headed. Instead, when we went inside, Pat walked up to the Delta ticket desk and asked for two tickets to Vegas. I made the instant decision to go, but I didn't want my customer to pay for my ticket, so I threw my credit card on the counter to pay for mine.

We flew to Vegas, had dinner, and hit the tables. About 1:00 a.m., while at the craps table, Pat looked over and said, "I liked the tie-in ad. We will do it just like the mock-up."

Around 3:00 or 4:00 a.m., we got back on the plane. Our flight out had done a turnaround in Los Angeles, and the same crew was taking it back to Dallas. One of the flight attendants stopped us. "Didn't you fellows just get off of this plane?"

Pat told her, "Yeah, we didn't like it."

We got back to the Adolphus Hotel shortly before 7:00 a.m., and I was, of course, wearing the same clothes I'd worn the day before. Pat told me the hotel gift shop sold dress shirts and ties. I dropped him off, bought a shirt and tie, and stopped at a service station to change on my way to work. I went straight to see my boss, David Lamb, and told him the whole story, not sparing him any details. David was thrilled that I had a natural rapport with Pat, a man who had avoided Kodak management for years. He was, however, a bit concerned about my methods—especially since Vegas was not in our division's ten-state territory.

"Jay," he said, "were you drunk when you decided to go to Vegas with Pat?"

"No. We enjoyed a few drinks, but I wasn't drunk."

"Did you put the flight on your Kodak Air Travel credit card?"

"No! See, I told you I wasn't drunk."

I seized the opportunity to jump on a plane with a client, even though it defied most corporate people's idea of logic and was a risky decision. It was a spur-of-the-moment opportunity that required a quick decision. Most corporate junior executives wouldn't have made that same decision, but a lot of entrepreneurs might. Entrepreneurs are just different. They have to be able to take measured and calculated risks.

Today I coach entrepreneurs to become all they can be. I have a glass conference room table that has etchings of major deals I've participated in sandblasted right into the table. It's a great reminder, as we sit around this table and talk, of the various lessons I've learned along the way. The logo of one company that I invested in and suffered a big loss is embedded in an ugly dark cloud to remind me of a mistake I won't make again.

Entrepreneurs come to the table for many reasons. Some are in trouble, some need a sounding board, others need to have the available options pointed out to them, and some are starting a new venture and need guidance. Who shows up? The ones who ask.

Entrepreneurs ask.

I mentor them, and when I truly realized how big the need was, I started an organization called Biz Owners Ed (BizOwnersEd.org) to help support entrepreneurs. At Biz Owners Ed, each entrepreneur has the opportunity to share and can discuss business challenges with expert mentors. It's a great forum where entrepreneurs get together for four hours once a week for ten consecutive weeks, experience presentations from extremely successful entrepreneurs and guest speakers, and receive personal mentoring. I think every city should have a chapter or an organization like it to help support entrepreneurs and help them discover the answers to the questions they are asking.

I love learning from others—another trait of entrepreneurs. I wholeheartedly believe that you can learn what you don't know in order to become successful.

Entrepreneurs do what it takes to accomplish the goal.

Sometimes things don't always go as you planned. My dad had a major financial setback shortly before I went to college.

He was in his late sixties when the arrival of television devastated his small-town movie theater business. He would've given me every dollar he had, but I felt like his plate was full enough without helping to fund my college education. Starting college at the age of seventeen and financing my higher education often called for some creativity.

I saw no reason to spend four years accomplishing what I could in three and a half with no summer school. It meant the degree would cost me less. I used to have a quote from Rudyard Kipling on my bedroom dresser mirror that said, "He travels the fastest who travels alone." I was eager to get out of school and into the real world.

My plan to pay for college started when I was fourteen. My family had just moved to Omaha, Nebraska, and I began searching for a summer job around town. After a frustrating day of rejections, I finally gave up and went to a movie. I sat down next to a girl about my age, and we began talking. I told her about my love of horses, and she told me about riding every summer at the nearby YWCA Camp Brewster. I thanked her, left the theater, and—in less than an hour—was sitting at the YWCA office talking with the director.

Camp Brewster was owned and run for half the summer by the YWCA. The remainder of the summer, the Jewish Community Center (JCC) leased and operated the facility. I got a job from the YWCA working in the horsemanship program and spent the first half of the summer as the only guy at an all-girls' camp. While working at the YWCA camp, I contacted the Jewish Community Center and was hired to work for their riding program the second half of the summer as the only gentile on the camp staff. Fortunately, they had not been able to find a Jewish cowboy.

The second year, I was allowed to provide three of the horses each organization leased for the riding program. After my third year,

I was contracted to direct the horsemanship program and provide all the horses. My summer earnings at Camp Brewster and the JCC camp provided a significant portion of the funds I needed to attend college.

I started college in the fall following high school graduation and attended the University of Iowa. My plan called for carrying twenty to twenty-one hours a semester and to graduate in seven semesters with no summer classes. I also needed to work about thirty hours a week while in school, so it was important to get all my classes in the mornings. This allowed me to work in the afternoons and evenings.

To get all of my classes in the morning, creative thinking was required. Because registration times were assigned on a rotating basis each semester and the morning classes always filled up first, I knew that, somehow, I had to be at the front of the line each semester—regardless of that semester's alphabetical registration criteria. I showed up for my first semester's registration early carrying a tray I had liberated from the dorm's cafeteria and dressed in a sport coat and tie even though I didn't meet that semester's criteria for early registration. (Fortunately, this was before computers took over all our lives.) I located the coffee concession stand outside the secure registration area and bought a half dozen donuts and ten cups of coffee. With the tray loaded and my hands full, I headed for the staff entry gate.

The guard cleared the way and opened the gate for me. After I had been waved through by the gatekeeper, I passed out the coffee and pastries and proceeded to register for all of my classes. I used that same gimmick to register first every semester, except the two that alphabetically put me at the front of the line. I never had a class that wasn't over by 1:00 p.m. in my entire college career.

While living in a dormitory at the university, one day I noticed a well-dressed man in the lobby posting a sign on our dorm bulletin board. When he left, I walked over to the board. His sign announced that the tobacco company R.J. Reynolds needed a part-time helper to distribute sample tobacco products in dorms, sororities, and fraternities on campus. The sign said that he would be back in the dorm lobby at 4:00 p.m. the following Wednesday to interview applicants for the position. After looking over my shoulder, I removed the ad from the bulletin board. At 3:30 p.m. the following Wednesday, I replaced the sign on the bulletin board and appeared at 4:00 p.m. for the only interview. Amazingly, I got the job, and I spent the next three years distributing the freshest four-to-a-pack, wax-sealed cigarettes in existence all over campus.

I also worked part-time for an auto repair company aptly named You Smash 'Em, We Fix 'Em. We had three wreckers we called Baby Bear, Mama Bear, and Papa Bear. Papa Bear could pick up and haul anything on the road, and I had an anxious night or two hauling tractor-trailer rigs. The slow night shifts and weekends were great times to study while waiting for the phone to ring. I worked about thirty hours a week there.

I soon learned that there was money to be made in wrecked cars. Any time a student or faculty car was brought in with a broken front windshield, I removed the section of glass containing the campus parking permit from the windshield, methodically and carefully removed the sticker from the glass, and put it on a plastic sheet. There was a strong market for those stickers.

The University of Iowa's football coach, Forest Evashevski, produced great teams with a strong fan following. This made tickets scarce and brought prices above their cost. I bought tickets from people who were not going to the game during the week normally at cost or even below. I also bought tickets outside the stadium from people who had extras and were trying to sell them before entering the game. I marked them up and sold them outside the stadium. Scalping those game tickets also contributed to my education and finances.

In those days, hospitals would buy your blood, but they would only buy your blood once every eight weeks. However, there were two hospitals in Iowa City. I was therefore able to "donate" every four weeks for fifteen dollars a pint at one hospital and twenty-five dollars a pint at the other hospital. Yes, in those days I may have been a little too Machiavellian, but when the objective—in this case, a college degree—is important enough, you simply do what you have to do.

During my sixth semester, I was called into the Dean of Students' office. Someone had figured out that I had been forging an advisor's signature for the sign-off on my over-eighteen-hours schedule. I finally convinced the dean that it had been working well for a long time, and if I had to drop any hours, I could not graduate in seven semesters and would therefore have to drop out to earn more money. I did graduate after seven semesters, at the ripe old age of twenty.

(Just for the record, I stayed busy but had a hell of a lot of fun in college.)

Entrepreneurs are willing to do the things others won't do for a few years so that they can do the things others can't do for the rest of their lives.

Be different! When you play to win big, you won't win them all, but you won't get lost in the crowd. It may take a few trial-and-error moments before you figure out what makes you stand out.

As college graduation approached, I spent a lot of time preparing for on-campus interviews. I was completing college in seven semesters without summer school and was graduating in January. This meant there were fewer companies interviewing on campus than was the case for spring graduations. The two job offers that I was seriously considering when the interviews ended were with AT&T and Eastman Kodak. I still remember the AT&T interviewer, a very fine gentleman named Otto Steuck. Mr. Steuck said, "Jay, I'm going to make you a job offer despite the fact that I firmly believe that within seven or eight years, you'll be in the entrepreneurial world of small business."

The Kodak interviewer had left me with a form to fill out and suggested I accompany the form with a personal letter. In 1960, Kodak was riding high, had forty thousand employees worldwide, and was considered one of the best career opportunities available. I knew that my first impression would be of paramount importance, and that it would, of necessity, be made by the transmittal letter accompanying my application to the company.

I decided on a go-for-broke approach. At the top of the letter and in capital letters, I typed, "I CAN BRING MORE TO KODAK THAN A COLLEGE EDUCATION." And the opening line read, "While operating the south end of a north-bound pitchfork, I had a great deal of time for meditation." The letter went on to explain how, at age fourteen, I was a stable hand for both the YWCA's Camp Brewster south of Omaha, Nebraska, and the Jewish Community Center's camp at the same location the second half of the summer. By the last two summers in college, I furnished all the horses, instruction, and staff for both camps' riding programs. I went on to underline the statement, "I built a barn," and told how the camp needed a larger barn: YWCA thought that since the JCC camp was double the attendance of YWCA, the JCC should pay for it. The JCC felt YWCA should pay for it because they owned the property. I was able to negotiate a compromise where the two organizations shared the cost, and it was a win for all concerned.

I knew the letter would definitely get a reaction; I just wasn't sure if it would be good or bad. I was ecstatic when Kodak offered me one of only six slots in their two-year executive training program and told me that the advertising department had agreed to pick up my salary for the two years of the program. For the next two years, I floated from department to department, worked directly with top management in each setting, enjoyed working the Kodak pavilion at the 1964 New York World's Fair for three months, spent time working with the J. Walter Thompson Advertising Agency (now Wunderman Thompson) in New York City, and traveled extensively with the sales training department. In those days, Kodak sponsored the highly successful *The Ed Sullivan Show*. I was not a big fan of Ed Sullivan, but I learned one thing from him that I have never forgotten, and it has served me well: "Always put your best act on first."

After completing the program, I worked briefly in the advertising department and then took a leave of absence to complete my, at that time, mandatory military service.

Not long after returning to my job with Kodak at their Rochester, New York headquarters, I maneuvered a transfer to Kodak's ten-state southwest regional office in Dallas, Texas.

Otto was right. Seven and a half years later, having transferred to Dallas with Kodak, I turned in my resignation and opened Ranchland.

Don't overlook real estate as a great way to make money.

When I transferred to Dallas with Kodak, the first thing I did after settling in was buy a horse. I boarded my horse in what was then still a somewhat rural area on the north edge of Dallas, close to Addison Airport. When I went to ride one weekend morning, the owner of the property where I boarded my horse told me he was about to go look at a nearby eleven-acre piece of property he was thinking about buying. When he invited me to go along, I accepted.

The tract contained a house, servant quarters (which hadn't been occupied for several years), a horse barn, a separate stud barn, a lighted arena, and an Ford 8N tractor used to mow the property—in short, a nice piece of property. A few weeks later, I asked my friend what had come of his efforts to buy that property. He informed me that he had decided not to pursue the purchase. I immediately went over, talked to the owner, and discovered that the owner wanted $76,000 (1966 pricing) for the land, buildings, tractor, and all. Because I was young and had no money, I began to plan how I could come up with the down payment.

I contacted my dad, who a few years earlier had narrowly avoided bankruptcy in the theater business that had been rendered unprofitable by the arrival of television in rural Iowa. Dad wrote me a poignant letter, indicating that he was pleased to be able to help me at a time in my young life when his help would still be meaningful. He mortgaged his just paid off $16,000 home for the $12,000 I needed. It's an enormous advantage in life to have someone who believes in you. I knew that, no matter what happened, I could make the $83.96 monthly payments on his loan.

I then called my close friend at Kodak, George, and told him I had located a property that we needed to buy. He agreed to go fifty-fifty and put up his $12,000. George and I began a series of unsuccessful efforts with local lenders and banks to secure the loan necessary for us to buy the property. After still another failed attempt, I optimistically told George that I thought we should call our new property the GJ Ranch, with "G" standing for George and "J" standing for me.

George said, "I like it, because if this doesn't work I can always say, 'Gee, Jay, how did we get ourselves into this mess?' "

We finally secured our loan and closed on the property. I cleaned up the long-abandoned servants' cottage and moved in to cut my expenses. The rent we received on the main house almost covered our mortgage payments. Eighteen months later, we sold the property for $200,000. Our profit was the seed money for a still larger dream: Ranchland.

Keep the momentum going. Always learn, be proactive, and be willing to make a move.

The one who makes the most moves often wins, because, as the saying goes, "You can't make any of the shots you don't take." You can't win if you don't make a move. Entrepreneurs are always thinking and always taking action.

Once I had some capital and a regular Kodak paycheck, I began to pursue my dream of owning acreage away from the city where I worked. A fellow member of the Shriners' Black Horse Patrol who lived northwest of Dallas invited me and my horse out to ride one weekend. When I arrived, he was finishing a project, so I decided to ride out alone for a while. As I was riding, I approached a stock pond and there encountered a man in bib overalls with a two-day growth of beard, a fishing pole, and a beer.

As I got closer, he said, "That's about the prettiest horse I ever saw. I'll trade you this fishing pole for your horse."

I figured he was a local hired hand, and—without another word spoken—I dismounted, took his fishing pole and his beer, and he rode off on my horse. He returned about thirty minutes later and exclaimed that he had not been on a horse in over twenty years and had never been on one that was so well mannered or handled so smoothly.

We struck up a conversation, and I learned that he owned 240 acres, including the land we were standing on. I told him my friend had a few acres near him, and I was looking to buy land in the area. We agreed that next Saturday I would bring two horses, and we would ride over his land together. My parting words were, "When we ride out of your woods next weekend, I want to own some of your land."

The following Saturday when our ride was over, I did. Specifically, it was an eighty-acre tract that was somewhat set apart from his other land. I agreed to purchase the eighty acres for $72,000, 70 percent of which he agreed to carry on a note. I carved out the back ten acres for my homestead and sold the remaining seventy acres in two-and-a-half to fifteen-acre tracts so quickly that I was able to pay off his note in less than a year. I then began work on the house that I had been building in my mind for many years.

Yes, I was extra lucky, but even if the fisherman had been a local hired hand, I could have learned a lot from him.

Don't prejudge people and miss out on the wisdom they can share.

Entrepreneurs always find a way. Sometimes it's not the normal way or the way everyone else does it, but they find a way to make things happen in their favor.

One weekend when I was out working at my house's construction site, a neighbor—whom I had not met, but who owned the ranch adjacent to my property—came by. He introduced himself as Bob and asked how the project was coming along. He invited me to have dinner with him and his wife.

"I'm hot and dirty," I said.

He said that I was his size and that he would lay some clothes out in the cabana at their pool. I decided to go.

Some of the best decisions are last minute. I jumped into the pool, cooled down, took a quick shower, dressed, and joined them for dinner.

Bob told me over dinner how he had been the number two man at the southwest division of Sears, and he had been operating this ranch as his transition into retirement. He was now ready to sell his 165-acre ranch, move with his wife to Sedona, Arizona, and really retire. He was asking $330,000 for the ranch. (Money was worth a great deal more in the 1960s.)

The land had a magnificent ranch house—complete with a pool and cabana, a clean, modern two-bedroom foreman's house, and an outstanding horse barn with a finished office, a covered porch, ten box stalls, and many amenities. The property also had two smaller out-buildings and a huge hay barn.

Because he saw me as a kid and not as a prospective buyer, he confided in me that, if necessary, he would throw in his herd of thirty mother cows with calves by their sides, two tractors, the farm equipment, and a pickup truck. When I casually inquired, Bob told me he wanted a solid deal, so he would have to get $50,000 down, but he would be happy to carry a 6 percent note for the $280,000 balance.

When I thanked Alice and Bob Carr (ABC Ranch) for a lovely meal and evening, I was trying to play it calm and cool, but my head was spinning. I got to town about 9:00 p.m. and immediately grabbed a legal pad and pen. Sometimes, you have to get creative, especially if you don't have capital.

By 2:00 a.m., I had laid out the business plan for the ranch. Additionally, I had a three-page list of potential investors, which consisted primarily of my fellow Kodak employees and my Kodak customers. The ranch would host corporate convention groups, company meetings, and employee picnics. For two four-week sessions each year, the ranch would be exclusively devoted to a youth horsemanship program.

My business plan called for raising $170,000 to make the down payment, build the bunk houses, launch the business, and reach cash flow positive.

Three nights after my dinner with Bob and Alice, with money raised, I knocked on their door, contract in hand. The Carrs were, to say the least, shocked. A rumor was soon circulating among the locals that some young kid had lost his mind and paid $2,000 per acre for 165 acres. (Less improvements, cattle, and personal property, I figured it was about $1,200 per acre.)

Today, more than fifty-four years later, land in this area is selling from a low of $60,000 per acre to a high of well over $100,000 per acre.

In any event, my dream of Ranchland had become reality—but it wouldn't have happened if I hadn't gotten creative in finding solutions to buy it.

When I purchased the ranch, I knew Bob was willing to throw in a herd of cattle and their calves. I also knew I would need all the pastureland for horses, but the herd of cattle was worth around $15,000; so I made sure they were included in the offer. Although we received a couple of bids from local buyers, we ended up shipping the cattle to the Fort Worth stockyards, which was still going strong at the time.

Not long after I moved out to the ranch, I purchased two horses from John Price. John was a mechanic at the Chevrolet dealership, but his passion was trading horses and ranching. He delivered the horses as I was writing his check, and I said, "John, I have to buy at least sixty more horses, and I just can't afford to pay as much as I'm giving you for these two for the rest of them."

John said, "Well, what are you going to do about that?"

My answer was, "I'm going to hire you as my foreman, and you're going to buy them."

John was with me until I sold the ranch and was one of the best hires I ever made.

He always represented me well. A couple of years after we sold the cattle, I was in Denton, Texas, at the feed store—the only customer there at that moment—and the owner started visiting with me. He told me that when I was trying to sell the herd of cattle, John came in to pick up some feed at the same time as a cattle buyer who had made an offer on my herd. The cattle buyer asked John, "Is your boss going to accept my offer and sell me the cattle?"

John's response was, "I don't rightly think so." When asked why, John said, "My boss don't know a lot about cattle, but he knows a lot about money."

Sometimes it's easier and more profitable to change the players than to change the game.

As a boy, I always enjoyed pinball machines. My enjoyment of them caused me to think about how the owners of the machines made money with them. I observed the machines in establishments and noticed that the vending machine companies changed out the machines periodically. Because my experience with them caused me to know there was nothing wrong with the machines, I wondered what the reason was for the change and all the effort that change entailed. In observing further, I noticed a correlation between the length of time a machine was present in an establishment and the number of people who played the machine. The longer a machine was there, the less the patrons played it. So, I decided that the most profitable pinball machine business would avoid the expense of frequent rotation of the machines. I concluded that an airport was the ideal place for a pinball concession, because there it's the people who change; there's no need to change the machines.

I acquired the pinball concession at the DFW Airport. Actually, I convinced Dobbs House to let me put a machine in each of their twenty-four cocktail lounges scattered in various DFW terminals. I took half, and they took half. I enjoyed trucking quarters to the bank until I sold the venture at a handsome profit.

— 2 —

Giving and Taking Advice

While at Kodak, I joined the military, knowing that with my lottery number, I would be drafted anyway. I did a six-month stint on active duty in the army, then joined a National Guard unit and did one weekend each month and two weeks each summer for the next six years to complete my obligations. I was stationed by the army for most of my six months of active duty at Fort Sill near Lawton, Oklahoma. Roy, one of my Kodak customer contacts, lived in Oklahoma City, and I spent many weekends as a guest of Roy and his wife. After my army service ended and I had transferred to Dallas with Kodak, Roy called to ask if I had $10,000 to invest in an oil deal he was going to invest in. I had $6,000, which I had saved to build a house in the countryside north of Dallas, but I wanted to invest with Roy. My bank agreed to loan me the additional $4,000. By the time I was to write my check, Roy's driller had already struck oil. I took the drilling logs to the bank, and the bank agreed to lend me the entire $10,000 for my investment. I preserved the $6,000 originally dedicated for the down payment on my house.

I received royalty checks on that oil well for over forty years, and to this day, I have never even seen the well.

A few years ago, I decided to travel to southwestern Wyoming with two of my horses and ride in the desert surrounding Little America, where I had lived during my youth. Because I was taking my horses, I called ahead to the local sheriff's department, got the sheriff on the line, and asked for his advice concerning where I might board my horses while there.

He gave me the name of Dale, the foreman of the Broad Bent Ranch. When I called Dale, he agreed to stable my horses and provide a hook-up at the ranch for my horse trailer with living quarters. After I arrived and settled in, and not wanting to overstep my welcome, I asked Dale if there were any places I should avoid.

"I don't think that's a problem," Dale replied. "The ranch is a million acres, and we're standing right in the middle of it." Enough said.

Over the coming days, I came to greatly respect Dale's knowledge of ranching and horses. When I was leaving, I told him that I was looking to buy two horses, and, if he ran across a couple he thought I might like, I would appreciate his buying them for me.

Some weeks later, I received a call from Dale. He had purchased two horses for me at a total cost of less than $2,000. I told him I would make arrangements for their shipment to Texas. Once I had received an $836 quote for the shipment, I called Dale and offered to pay that amount of money to him if he and his wife wanted a short vacation in Texas. He did, and he and his wife spent some time with Bettye (my wife) and me at our home in rural North Texas.

My neighbors were more than impressed with Dale's judgment of horseflesh. After I initially resisted, I sold one of the horses for $6,000 and, ten years later, sold the other one for $18,750. I was willing to take Dale's horses sight unseen because I had bet on Dale, and I received a sizable return on my bet as my reward.

Oh yes, I did send Dale a thank you note with a $1,000 check enclosed.

You do not always need all the facts or eyes on the investment to make the right decisions. In order to win, bet on winners. In most transactions, you are betting primarily on people. Follow your gut feelings.

When I transferred to Dallas with Kodak, I had an assistant named Shirley. She and her husband, Pete, were originally from the rural Quitman, Texas, area, and both sets of their parents still lived there. Shirley and Pete wanted to buy land near Quitman that in time they could build on and retire. To that end, they spent most weekends traveling there to look at available real estate. One Monday morning, I walked into the office and wasn't certain if Shirley was excited or depressed. It seems that, over the weekend, she and Pete had finally found the ideal piece of property: a one-hundred-acre tract in two parcels separated by a road through the property. Eighty acres lay on one side of the road, and twenty acres lay on the other side. Unfortunately, the owner would sell only the entire one-hundred-acre tract. He was willing to take 20 percent down and a long term note at a very fair interest rate. Even stretching to their limit, they could afford only the eighty-acre parcel. Shirley was perplexed and asked if I had any thoughts as to a solution to their problem.

"Shirley!" I said. "You don't have a problem. I will buy the twenty acres. The seller will be happy to sell the parcels separately as long as they close simultaneously, and he doesn't have to worry about ending up with one parcel. What's more, I want you to understand that I am not doing you a favor. You are doing me one."

Shirley was aghast. "You haven't even seen the property," she said.

"I know," I responded. "But you've been looking at real estate in that area most every weekend for months. Both of your families know land values there. Road frontage adds value, and the twenty acres has four times as much frontage per acre as the eighty. Rural land in large parcels typically sells for less money per acre than it does in small parcels. You will get the land you want, and I will have a great investment."

The seller was happy to take our separate notes as long as we did a simultaneous closing, assuring that the entire one hundred acres sold at the same time. Shirley had her dream property; I didn't even see the property until a year later. When I sold it less than two years later, the buyer found me. I paid no commission and sold for more than double my purchase price . . . and I will always be Shirley's white knight.

Don't be afraid to give, or get, tough advice.

I frequently tell people that all my friends are strong because the weak can't handle me. I have often thought about trying to soften my somewhat overly direct and harsh style, but I always conclude with, "Why the hell would I want a bunch of weak friends?"

When Tony Jeary and I were collaborating to write *Advice Matters*, one afternoon Tony turned to me and said, "Jay, you could make big bucks as a coach."

My reply was, "Yes, but then I would need to be nice to people just because they have a big checkbook." I know myself well enough to know that I cannot candy coat the truth, and I am much better at tough love than playing nice.

One example of my style of tough love occurred several years ago when I was serving on a Denton, Texas grand jury. During a break, I was surprised when one of the jurors, Jane, asked me if I would be willing to help her with her business. When I inquired as to why she asked me, she told me that three people had suggested that I was the one she needed to approach for help.

As is my custom, I agreed to have one session at my office. I always use initial sessions to gather the facts and decide if I can be of help and, if so, whether I want to become involved. Jane had operated a very successful cake-and-candy business for over twenty years. Her primary focus was wedding cakes. Over the past three years, her profits had dwindled to near nonexistent, and Jane had reached the point of hating to get up and go to work.

We had a good meeting, and I agreed to sign on. One of Jane's first questions was how much I charged. I explained that normally I did not charge; however, in her case, it would cost her candy and cake.

At our next meeting, I had studied her overall operations and financials and concluded that step one was for her to raise her prices. When I told her she immediately needed to raise her prices by 20 percent, she protested that she would lose all of her customers. My response was that she had sought me out because she was slowly going broke and, half-jokingly, told her, "Let's get it over with." When she left my office, she had agreed to raise her prices 20 percent across the board.

She did lose a small number of customers, but with the additional 20 percent of revenue hitting her bottom line, she again became profitable almost overnight. She arrived for our third session absolutely elated and said, "Oh, Jay, you were right. I'll do anything you tell me."

I told her that step two was not going to be as easy. And again, she said, "I'll do anything."

I explained that an employee who had been with her from day one had to go. This employee was creating a lot of problems, and the final straw was that the employee had involved her new husband somewhat in the business. Amidst the flow of emotion and tears, Jane finally asked, "Is there a compromise?"

She immediately brightened up when I said, "Of course." The smile faded when I explained that as long as she dismissed the employee, banned her from the premises, and changed the locks (if she wanted to), she could continue to send the employee a check. Jane reluctantly accepted my advice and dismissed the employee. Several months later, she confided that this second piece of advice had been even more valuable than raising her prices.

Several years have now passed. Jane remains profitable, has expanded her business, and we remain good friends. I'm delighted with her success and glad that I was able to help. As I was preparing to publish this book, I sent a draft of this story to Jane for her approval and permission to include it. Below is her response:

I loved it just the way you wrote it. You could also say that when I saw your name on caller ID, I broke into a sweat for the first few years. When I talk about you, I tell people that I never ask you anything unless I want the truth, and sometimes the truth is not what I want to hear but what I need to hear.

You truly changed my life, and more specifically, my business life. Thanks for that. I love and respect you and Bettye so much.

Jane

Know when to use The Gimmick

After buying the ranch and preparing for the summer youth horsemanship program, one of the high priorities on my to-do list was to find the perfect individual to head the horsemanship instruction program. It was my good fortune to negotiate with Darrell Davidson to fill that slot. Darrell was college-educated, an outstanding horse trainer, and quarter horse judge by choice. Darrell and I spent a good deal of time together preparing for the youth ranch programs. One weekend, he invited me to join him when he was going to a quarter horse show that he had been hired to judge. It was a big show, a hot day, and Darrell never got a break from the time it started at 8:00 a.m. until the lunch break at noon. In a class he judged shortly before noon, he had placed a young lady in second place, and the father became a bit irate. Dad was used to his daughter placing first and accused Darrell, quite loudly, of being a lousy judge.

At noon after a tough morning, we walked back to the truck, dropped the tailgate, sat down, and prepared to enjoy the lunch we had packed. We had just relaxed and started to eat when Dad found us. Once again, he started berating Darrell and said, "It isn't right. It just isn't right."

With that, Darrell set down his sandwich and replied, "It may not be right, but it's damn sure official."

Driving back to the ranch that evening, I was still laughing when I told Darrell that was what I always called, "using The Gimmick." He inquired as to what I meant by The Gimmick. I explained to him that when the situation merited it, I always responded with the whole truth and nothing but the truth, so help me God—that was what I called my Gimmick.

Over the following years, we became close friends, partnered on several business ventures, and bought and sold numerous horses. When the situation called for it, one of us would simply say to the other, "Let's use The Gimmick."

On one occasion, Darrell and I were sitting in the ranch office waiting for the arrival of a young lady who had attended the summer youth ranch. She was coming with her parents to look at a liver chestnut quarter horse gelding that was certified as a Reining Register of Merit winner, meaning that he had received at least ten points in registered quarter horse shows. We had recently purchased the horse from the prior owner because she was leaving for college.

Despite all the horse's pluses, it had one abnormality: its left eye was set at least an inch lower on his head than his right eye. While we waited, I suggested to Darrell that perhaps we should use The Gimmick and point out this defect when they arrived. Darrell said he was happy to do so, but that I should consider the fact that we purchased the horse well below market price and were selling it with a very reasonable markup. Because the buyers were not professional horsemen, they might put too much weight on this defect and reject the horse. If that happened, by the time we located and purchased an equally talented horse, we might well have to charge twice the price we had placed on this horse. Before I could digest his thinking, the family pulled up—complete with Mom, Dad, Grandpa, and Grandma.

We all walked down to the barn together where the horse was saddled and waiting. Darrell led it out to the arena, stepped aboard, and ran a flawless reining pattern on it. We then had the young lady mount up, and she, too, ran a perfect pattern. I led the horse back toward the barn with the entire family close at hand and Dad ready to write the check. I finally maneuvered the conversation around to where Dad asked if there was anything I didn't like about the horse. When I said there was something I did not like about the way its eyes set on its head, Darrell had to go around the corner of the barn to avoid being heard laughing. With that, Mom, Dad, Grandpa, and Grandma all stood directly in front of the horse, yet—to this day I don't know why—none of them seemed to notice the defect. At that point, I simply said, "Let's go up to the office. You can write the check while I fill out the owner transfer papers."

— 3 —

Always Ask

Having maneuvered a transfer from Kodak's headquarters in Rochester, New York, to Dallas, Texas, I began making preparations to relocate. I called my friend, George—the Kodak advertising representative with whom I would share responsibility for the ten-state southwest region.

George asked, "Does your car have air conditioning?"

Although I was the proud owner of a sporty Ford Thunderbird, I had to answer, "No."

George responded, "You'll never be able to sell a luxury car in Texas if it isn't air-conditioned."

My promotion included a company car when I got to Texas, but I had planned to drive my Thunderbird there and then sell it. Instead, I needed to sell my car while still in New York.

From that moment forward, I asked every single person I encountered, "Do you want to buy a Thunderbird?" I even prepared a selling sheet that I carried with me and handed out. I had begun to fear that I would have to accept the low wholesale offer I had received for my car and ship my personal possessions to Texas.

Three nights before I was scheduled to leave for Dallas, I went to the laundromat at about midnight to do some laundry. When I walked in, the janitor was mopping the floor. As I had done with every other person I had encountered, I said, "Would you like to buy a Thunderbird?"

He stopped mopping, leaned on his mop, and said, "I've always wanted to own a Thunderbird."

He drove a Studebaker Golden Hawk that the highway department's ice-and-snow-control chemicals had almost rusted to the ground. I had padded my asking price by about $400, so I allowed him $400 for his car, and we closed the deal the next day.

Two days later, I loaded all my possessions in the Studebaker and headed for Texas, with Kodak paying me twelve cents a mile.

I could see the highway through the floorboards, and every hundred miles I had to add brake fluid through another opening in the floorboard. While I had doubts about whether this car would make it from New York to Dallas, I figured that I could always push it into the ditch and catch the bus.

I made it all the way to Dallas in that Studebaker and pocketed Kodak's twelve cents a mile. Then, I picked up my company car and sold the Studebaker for twenty dollars.

Ask. There are hundreds, if not thousands, of wonderful happenings that have occurred throughout my personal and professional life simply because I always ask.

After I raised the money to buy Ranchland and create my youth summer ranch/horsemanship venture and corporate dude ranch, my next challenge was making the youngsters (and, more importantly, their parents) aware of its existence so they sign up for one or both of the two four-week summer sessions. I had little money for marketing and public relations; time was running short, and enrollments were coming far too slowly. Sitting at my desk while contemplating my first major failure and bankruptcy at the ripe old age of twenty-eight, I was flipping through the *Western Horseman* magazine (the world's most popular and widely circulated horse magazine at the time) and noticed the magazine's masthead. It listed Dick Spencer III as the publisher, along with the magazine's address in Colorado Springs, Colorado, and phone number. On impulse, I picked up the phone and dialed the number. When the receptionist answered, I asked to speak to Mr. Spencer. Lo and behold, I was connected, and a pleasant voice said, "What can I do for you?"

I said, "Mr. Spencer, I'm opening a summer youth horsemanship ranch north of Dallas-Fort Worth (DFW) and am coming to Colorado Springs to take you to lunch and tell you about it. I called to find out when you would like me to be there."

We had lunch the following week. The magazine did a color spread followed by numerous continued columns and a total of sixteen photos.

As a result of the article, our summer youth ranch was a booming success and enrolled boys and girls from thirty-eight states. That fall, Dick sent the editor, Chuck King, down to participate in a four-day, extended weekend, adult horsemanship course we offered. His attendance generated another great article that helped fill several adult horsemanship clinics. The corporate dude ranch/meeting facility we operated the other ten months of the year also became very successful, and I was able to remove bankruptcy from my list of upcoming events.

The principle of Ask and Ye Shall Receive served me well during the marketing and building of Ranchland.

Most of my Ranchland investors and the board of directors were former fellow employees of Kodak and Kodak customers. These were friends with whom I had close relationships.

At a board meeting, I read a draft of the copy I had prepared for the youth ranch brochure. When I read that Jim Shoulders, sixteen-time world champion rodeo cowboy, would visit the ranch during each of the two sessions to personally meet and visit with the youngsters, one of the board members who fully appreciated Jim's fame and celebrity status stopped me and said, "Jay, how in the world did you get Jim Shoulders to agree to come to the ranch?"

"I haven't," I told him. "In fact, I've never met or spoken to the man, but I think his presence and endorsement will be a major plus, and I'm sure going to try to make it happen."

The following week, I called Jim at his Oklahoma ranch. He agreed to visit with me, and I drove up for the meeting. Jim agreed not only to visit each session at the ranch but to also attend the press party that announced our summer youth horsemanship program and our corporate offerings to the DFW market. His presence ensured us a great turnout. Knowing that we were a struggling startup, Jim refused to accept any compensation for his support. (In those days, even the top rodeo cowboys didn't make big money.) Thanks to Jim, over seventy members of the media attended, and we received outstanding coverage.

There are a lot of nice people out there, and a lot of people who are willing to be helpful; but they can't say yes if you don't ask them. If you're not good at asking for things, maybe you need to be.

I was very gratified a few years later to learn that Jim had been in an incredibly successful Miller Beer TV commercial. When I ran into my friend Neil Gay, the owner of the Mesquite Rodeo in Texas, he told me the details of the Miller Beer TV commercial story. Jim got a call from an advertising executive in New York City. The exec said, "Jim, I'm calling to see if you would be interested in being in a Miller Beer commercial we're about to produce."

Jim replied that he'd be interested, but there were a couple of hurdles they would need to get over. The advertising executive asked what those would be.

Jim said, "Well, first, there are thousands of young people who look up to me, and I promised myself that I wouldn't take part in anything that wasn't in good taste."

The advertising executive responded that Miller Beer was very sensitive in that area, and he was *absolutely* certain that it wouldn't be a problem. He assured Jim he would have the right to reject anything he was uncomfortable with. The executive then asked about the second hurdle.

Jim said, "Of course, that would be the money."

The executive explained that the money Jim received would be based on the number of times the commercial was shown in each market and the size of those markets. He concluded by saying, "However, in the event—for whatever reason—we never use the commercial at all, you would receive a check for $12,000."

Jim simply said, "Well, now that we're over that hurdle . . ."

As it turns out, that commercial was so popular and ran so long that Jim's compensation for that one commercial was greater than several years of his rodeo income—if not all of it.

Ask and you shall receive.

During the 1974 summer youth horsemanship program at Ranchland, two of the young ranchers who attended persuaded their parents to purchase the horse I had assigned them during the program. One young lady lived in Georgia, and the other in Florida. As part of the sale, I had agreed to deliver both horses after the second four-week program ended. Mark Patterson, my youth Ranch program director, and two counselors, Tom Woodson and Rusty Daniel, all lived on the East Coast and had asked to ride with me on their way home.

At that time, the only trailer I had on the ranch was a large stock trailer. I was far from excited about dragging it all the way to the East Coast and then pulling it back to Texas empty. As I was browsing through a newly arrived *Western Horseman* magazine, I saw a very impressive ad for Miley Horse Trailers. Although the Miley company went out of business long ago, at that time, they made the very finest horse trailer in the market and manufactured them in Fort Worth, Texas. In keeping with my belief that if you don't ask, no one can say yes, I called Miley's Fort Worth number and asked to speak to the general manager. When he came on the line, I introduced myself and asked him, "Do you have a two-horse trailer on your lot that should be in Florida?"

Glory be! He did. He gave me the name and phone number of the lady who purchased the trailer. I then called her and offered to deliver her trailer for less than she had expected to pay. I lined the walls of the trailer with heavy cardboard to ensure it arrived in pristine condition. We had a most enjoyable trip to Florida, stopped in Georgia to deliver one horse, delivered the second in Florida, and then went to the car wash with the trailer and delivered it to the owner. As absolute frosting on the cake, the father of our young Florida rancher volunteered to make his plane and pilot available to fly the four of us to the Bahamas for two days of R&R. When we got back to Florida, Mark, Tom, and Rusty headed to their respective homes; and I enjoyed a pleasant drive back to the ranch with a lot of cash in my pocket, a smile on my face, and no trailer in tow.

As mentioned before, great things happen when you ask.

While I was operating the Ranchland summer youth horsemanship ranch, Gordon McClendon (builder of a national communications empire) had Cielo Ranch near me just north of Dallas. One wing of the main ranch house was the John Wayne suite. I frequently provided horses when Gordon had more guests than his stable could accommodate. As a result, I was invited to a major party at Cielo Ranch the night before John Wayne's movie *Chisum* premiered in Dallas. I was standing near the pool when John stepped out of his quarters and was immediately surrounded by guests. As luck would have it, I ended up standing directly in front of John, not much more than an arm's length away. When there was a momentary silence, I looked up, and said, "Mr. Wayne, I've got to talk to you."

The legend replied, "Speak on, little man."

"I've got fifty youngsters who want to meet you," I said, and told him about our youth ranch.

Although obviously tipsy, he immediately replied, "Well, bring 'em to our parade in the morning, and I'll meet them."

I immediately headed back to my ranch, and by 4:00 a.m., had arranged to haul seventy head of horses and a surrey with a fringe on top complete with a sign welcoming Mr. Wayne to Dallas. With my staff and all the youngsters in their Ranchland logo shirts, we stood along the parade route while I wondered if he imbibed so much the night before that he wouldn't even remember our conversation.

About that time, a Cadillac convertible came by heading to the nearby start of the parade. When John Wayne saw our group, he tapped the driver on the shoulder, had him do a U-turn, and pulled up to the curb next to us. He got out, shook every single youngster's hand, then called a parade official over and instructed him that he wanted half of our group in front of his car and half of the group behind it. It sure is nice to find out that *some legends . . .* really are.

If you don't ask for what you want, you won't get what you want.

I wouldn't be able to tell this story now if I'd been too timid to approach John Wayne.

No one says yes to a question that you do not ask.

Sometimes you shouldn't believe what others tell you about their bottom lines, or about the bottom lines of other people. My Ranchland partner, Darrell, and I frequented a coffee shop in Denton where the locals got together to enjoy morning coffee and exchange stories (i.e., swap lies). At one of those sessions, we heard a tale about a local builder we knew named Joe who badly needed to sell an auto repair shop he owned and was leasing to a local mechanic. Times were hard in the real estate business, and interest rates were in excess of 18 percent. Joe was in a liquidity crunch. The locals were adamant that Joe was selling the building way too cheap, but the deal had to be 100 percent cash at closing, and no one had that much cash.

Darrell and I believed that we could borrow the money necessary to buy Joe's property. Our bank looked at our proposal and agreed to lend all but $15,000 of the money needed. We went to Joe and told him we would buy his property, but that he would have to carry a $15,000 second lien note that would be subordinate to the bank's first lien note. Joe agreed. (Ask and you shall receive.) Joe had previously received a deposit and the last month's rent from his tenant. Those funds were deducted at closing from Joe's proceeds and credited to us. Darrell and I walked away from the closing with the deed and a $2,300 check in our pocket. Neither Darrell nor I ever put a single penny of our own money into this income property. We sold it three years later for a handsome profit.

Never take someone else's word about another's requirements to make a deal.

If you don't ask, you cannot receive.

In the early 1980s after several successful ventures, I was finally ready to build my dream house: a ranch house situated on the highest point in the area overlooking my ranch. I installed Kohler's Rochelle commodes in all the bathrooms and the matching bidet in the master. At that time, I think the Rochelle low silhouette toilet was the most expensive commode that Kohler offered. Because I served as my own general contractor on numerous building projects, I frequently attended the National Home Builder's show. Three or four years after the ranch house was complete, I was at the show in Vegas. When I entered the Kohler exhibit, I asked a representative the name of the top-ranking Kohler executive who was currently in the exhibit. He said, "Well, today, that would be Mr. Kohler." He motioned toward two gentlemen conversing, indicating that Mr. Kohler was the gentleman on the left.

I walked over and stood nearby while they finished their conversation. When the visitor turned to leave, I immediately stepped forward and said, "Mr. Kohler, I'd like to speak to you."

I explained to him that I had already had to replace the four Rochelle commode seats because the bright Texas sun streaming in through the windows had turned the seats a yellowish color, and the replacements were already beginning to turn yellow. It wouldn't have been a big deal, but even back in the 1980s, the wholesale price on these seats was well over $100 each. The Rochelle commodes were designed so that no other seats could substitute. I explained that, while the Texas sun was indeed extremely bright, a product that carried the Kohler name and an extremely high price tag should retain its bright white color indefinitely.

With that, Mr. Kohler reached into his pocket, pulled out a business card, and wrote on the back:

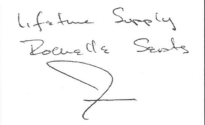

If you're not getting a lot of noes, you're missing a lot of yesses.

In 1995, my wife, Bettye, and I organized a tour of the Greek Isles and ancient Ephesus (near Kuşadasi, Turkey) with two dozen of our friends. Our commitment to attending a godchild's wedding in the United States necessitated our leaving the group a day early when we docked at Crete. Rough seas caused us to dock earlier than scheduled in Crete, so we arrived at the small airport about 11:00 a.m., and our flight to Athens wasn't until 7:00 p.m.

While standing near the Olympic Airline counter, I overheard the airline agent tell the couple ahead of me that, in addition to the 7:00 p.m. flight to Athens, they had one other, and it would depart in about forty-five minutes; however, there was only one seat available on that flight. The couple indicated that they would not be interested in traveling to Athens separately and would wait for the 7:00 p.m. flight.

When they left the ticket counter, I stepped up and was also told there was only one seat remaining on the early flight to Athens. I said, "That's perfect! My wife will take that last seat, and I'll take the jump seat in the cockpit." As I said this, I handed her my commercial pilot's license. (Please understand that the biggest plane I ever flew had ten seats.)

The wall behind the agent had a door and large plate glass windows that allowed us to see the 737 on the tarmac that would soon depart for Athens. The agent looked at my license, turned around, walked out onto the tarmac, and up the rolling stairs into the plane. She reappeared a minute or two later, and when she came back to the counter said, "That will be fine."

Bettye and I caught the early flight from Crete to Athens and made it home to the United States in time for the wedding. The pilots were great guys. They pointed out the sights to me and invited Bettye and me to dinner that evening.

This all happened because I did a little creative thinking and, more importantly, *asked*. Remember, the worst thing that can happen in situations like this is they say no. That leaves you even, not down.

Ask! A simple question can achieve great results. . . . It did in Tahiti.

Another time when Bettye and I were on our way to visit Australia and New Zealand, we stopped over in Tahiti. I decided it would be nice to rent a plane and see the sights topside. When I walked into the Fixed Base Operator (FBO) at the airport, there was another tourist in front of me standing at the counter. I overheard the manager telling him in order to rent a plane, it was required that you have a French pilot's license.

With that, the gentleman said, "In that case, do you have an instructor I can hire to fly with me so that I'll be legal?" The manager got on his radio, and an instructor walked into the room moments later. As they left to go preflight the plane, I walked up to the manager and told him I would like to rent a plane. He explained that I would need a French pilot's license. I simply asked, "What is involved in obtaining a French pilot's license?"

His reply was, "You need to go over to the building next door, show them your United States pilot's license, and pay them ten dollars."

On that same trip, we had previously stopped in Hawaii, and I had decided it would be nice to fly over several of the islands. When I went to the FBO, the owner explained that he was there alone and would have to give me a quick check flight before I could rent. Unfortunately, he was just minutes away from flying a parachutist up to altitude for a committed jump into a beach party. He'd be happy to give me the check flight when he returned. I simply said, "He's going to be in the back anyway. Why don't I sit up front, and after we throw him out, I can take my check right on the way down?" Worked out great, saved a lot of time, and we got to Maui in time for lunch.

Entrepreneurs have to be ready for opportunity; sometimes it doesn't knock twice.

A much more recent but excellent example of the power of asking is my story of getting acquainted with Norm Brodsky, coauthor of *Street Smarts*. My assistant at the time, Cari, worked her magic and came up with Mr. Brodsky's phone number. When I got him on the phone, we visited, and I told him that I very much wanted to take him to lunch.

"With you living in Texas and me in New York City, just when and where do you want to do that?" he asked.

"Absolutely anywhere and anytime that's convenient for you," I replied.

Three weeks later, David Hammer, cofounder of Biz Owners Ed—a program that teaches select business owners about how to scale and, ultimately, exit their businesses—and I flew to New York City, met Mr. Brodsky at his condominium next door to Trump Tower, and enjoyed an incredible two-and-a-half-hour lunch soaking up Norm's wisdom. In the process, I asked Norm if he would be willing to say a few words at the annual Biz Owners Ed (Biz) alumni luncheon in June and be the speaker for the Dallas chapter of the Entrepreneurs' Organization's dinner the following night at the George W. Bush Presidential Library and Museum. As frequently happens when you ask, Norm graciously accepted the invitation.

Both of Norm's presentations were outstanding. He drew the biggest crowd the Dallas chapter of the Entrepreneurs' Organization had attracted all year, blew away the attendees at our Biz Owners Ed luncheon, and presented Biz Owners Ed with a $5,000 donation check—thus becoming our first out-of-state mentor.

Use no as the starting point, not as the finish line.

When Bettye and I were approaching seventy, we were ready to change direction. So, in 2006, we sold our controlling interest in Smart Start to Lamar Ball, my handpicked successor, and another shareholder at a $15 million valuation. Smart Start was an ignition interlock device company that put a court-ordered unit on cars as a requirement for convicted DUI and DWI offenders to legally drive. The device required them to blow into a unit that would measure their breath alcohol content before the car would start.

I wrote to my friends who owned stock, advising them that we were selling out but that the company was headed to the moon, and I advised them to hold their stock. Lamar sold that business in 2015 for $340 million—all cash. I am the first to applaud Lamar's success in continuing to grow Bettye's and my goal of separating drinking from driving. We take great pride in having created many millionaires and several multi-millionaires among our friends, employees, and investors as a result of starting Smart Start. Hard to believe that when we ended the first month after opening, we had only one customer and sixty dollars in revenue.

With Smart Start behind us and the city pushing out to our ranch, we decided to move to town. We committed to buying a condominium unit in downtown Fort Worth. The project was still under construction as we were preparing to depart for Canada, the Calgary Stampede, and our extended annual summer vacation. Before leaving, I listed our ranch house north of Dallas-Fort Worth with a real estate agent. It was the summer of 2009, and the residential real estate market was truly in the tank. When we returned to Texas in late summer, one of the first things I did was call our real estate agent to get an update.

He informed me that the real estate market was dead and that he had only showed our place three times. He added that one of the couples who looked was really knocked out by the house, our hilltop location overlooking the Tour 18 golf course, and just about everything else. He went on to tell me that the prospects owned a home in Decatur, Texas, and had decided not to do anything until their current home was sold.

I asked my real estate agent for the name and phone number of the couple's real estate agent. I assured him that, per our listing contract, he would be paid as stipulated. However, I asked him to stay out of my way regarding this couple that he had long since written off as prospects.

My next step was to call the couple's real estate agent. She was happy to arrange for her clients to make another trip out to our ranch house. Before the day was out, we were scheduled to meet at our property the following day.

Less than forty-five minutes after Rick Garrett and his wife, Amy, arrived with their real estate agent, we agreed that they would be the proud new owners of our five-acre estate. I made some concessions, but none that my real estate agent should not have pursued had he been doing his job. I accepted a price below the asking price; however, my real estate agent was aware that I would accept a much lower price. My only other significant concession came as a result of knowing that Rick wanted to sell his house prior to buying another one.

I resolved this objection by suggesting that I give Rick a short term second loan in the amount of the equity he had in his present house. I agreed to make my loan at the lowest legal interest rate: at that time, about 1 percent. The note would be due at the earliest of either the closing date of the sale of his home or in two years. As it turned out, Rick followed my example, lowered the asking price on their Decatur home, and—as a result—sold and closed on his house in about five months.

Rick and I have become great friends, and he is one of Biz Owners Ed's valued mentors. I conduct all of my business so that, after the closing (be it the sale of real estate or a business), the buyer and I frequently develop an ongoing, friendly relationship. Many buyers of companies and other assets I have been involved in have become close friends.

That only happens when you live by a win-win philosophy.

None of this would have been possible had I simply accepted the no Rick gave my real estate agent as final.

Ask! When they say no, you are even; when they say yes . . . wow.

In 1999, my wife and I put together a cruise group composed of successful entrepreneurs. The common link was that all of us belonged to Joe Mancuso's nonprofit, The CEO Club. We belonged to chapters from various cities around the United States but had a great deal in common and were a close-knit group. We almost always cruised on a Crystal Cruises ship and, over the years, have taken at least twenty cruises. Typically, there would be about two dozen of us on any given cruise.

We were enjoying a great itinerary and were about three days out from our destination—Dover, England—when our butler shared interesting information: he told us that the largest penthouse on the ship had been under total renovation for the last two cruises, and all the work would be completed that day.

I immediately sought out the officer in charge of all hotel aspects of the ship. I suggested that because all our group were successful business owners, and typically half of them would book suites rather than staterooms, this would be a great opportunity to introduce our crowd to the finest penthouse suite on the ship. He asked when and how he might accommodate (accomplish) that. I said that the ideal answer was for the ship to host a fancy farewell party in the suite the evening before we disembarked in Dover. He agreed and arranged for the four butlers who were assigned to our group's suites to handle the bar and elaborate hors d'oeuvres. He then had invitations printed and delivered to each suite or stateroom occupied by our group members, inviting them to attend Jay and Bettye's Farewell Party.

I was on a roll and pushed my luck. During the cruise, I became acquainted with, spent a good deal of time with, and really enjoyed Bill Passo and his wife, Magic—a couple who was not in our group. (As I write this book, the real estate investment company Bill founded, Passco Companies LLC, has $3.9 billion assets under management.) I decided to add them to our farewell party guest list. Bill still gives me grief for my having a little fun as I addressed the invitation they received not to Mr. and Mrs. Bill Passo, but to "Magic Passo and guest."

I need to tell you the many marvelous things that have happened as a result of meeting Bill and Magic and inviting them to the farewell party:

1. Before we departed in Dover, I told Bill that when he had an investment he liked, I'd appreciate a call and an opportunity to participate. Nearly a year later, he called me when they were buying a major apartment complex that they were going to update, renovate, and resell. In about two years, my $400,000 investment returned a little over $600,000.

2. More importantly, the four of us enjoyed a river cruise from Memphis to New Orleans.

3. Bill and Magic joined Bettye and me for one of our twenty annual trips to the Calgary Stampede.

4. In 2022, Bill was able to facilitate my having a one-on-one, face-to-face meeting with Craig Hall. Craig, a self-made billionaire, has written two books on the importance of small business and entrepreneurs to the foundation and success of our country: *The Responsible Entrepreneur* and *Boom*. Both are well worth reading. Craig has most graciously agreed to present as a mentor at our nonprofit Biz Owners Ed program. Our mentors are by invitation only, must have built a megamillion-dollar company from a startup or stagnant company, and—as a token of their sincerity to give back— make a $5,000 donation to the nonprofit when they come aboard. Craig Hall qualifies on all counts several times over.

Having gathered and organized Joe Mancuso's CEO Club members for a cruise, Bettye and I affiliated with a travel agency, became certified travel agents, and announced the second cruise. There are numerous enjoyable benefits when you do it for real.

I asked myself: who gets paid for driving around the county every day?

When we launched one of our numerous companies, Healthcare Staff Resources, we originally staffed only pharmacists, but early on realized that we needed to add additional healthcare professionals and decided to expand our focus to include physical therapists (PTs) and occupational therapists (OTs). We recruited PTs and OTs from various countries, but the majority (fifty-two) came from the best school in the Philippines. We hired a company to handle the immigration details and paperwork. When they arrived, we initially arranged housing, taught many of them to drive and helped them get their driver's license, and helped them set up bank accounts. When they worked long enough for us to recover the cost of their immigration, we raised their pay to exactly what we paid United States therapists who worked with us. Because that was our policy, they told their friends about us who had come to the states with other companies that were underpaying their physical therapists. We had numerous, already-emigrated PTs join us at Healthcare Staff Resources.

One of our very first Filipino PT recruits was JoJo Sucgang. After her orientation, her first ninety-day assignment was to fill a slot under our contract with the Texas Department of Corrections. On a Sunday afternoon, she bused to Palestine, Texas. That evening, not long after Bettye and I had gone to bed, Bettye's phone rang. It was JoJo, and she was panicked. She told Bettye that after she checked into the motel, she tried to arrange tomorrow morning's transportation to the prison located a few miles out of town. Much to her chagrin, she had just found out that there was no taxi or other transportation service to the prison. Bettye told her to stay by the phone and we would call her back.

After waking up enough to ponder JoJo's problem for a few moments, I picked the phone up and called the Anderson County Sheriff's office in Palestine. I ask the deputy who answered for the name of and home number of the sheriff. When I dialed the sheriff's home, he personally answered the call. I explained the problem, and he very graciously agreed to have a deputy drive JoJo to the prison the following morning and have another deputy bring her back to Palestine when her shift was over. Not only did he provide that service for her first day's work, he provided her transportation for the entire ninety days of her assignment.

I may have mentioned it before: no one can say yes to requests you don't make.

— 4 —

Skip Some Mistakes; Move Forward Faster

If you've got a fantastic business idea and someone else agrees, it sure can be tempting to take their money and sell shares or bring them on as an investor in order to build it. Most entrepreneurs don't have sufficient savings to adequately capitalize their first business. I was no exception. However, I resisted the temptation to land the big, single investor with all the capital I would ever need. I resisted because the golden rule of business is "He who has the gold makes the rules."

Don't rush in to accepting investor money and get locked in to one investor.
If you do something for the money now, you might regret it later on.
Your ideal investors will bring more to the table than just money.

Instead of going after the one investor who could cover everything, I decided to raise the necessary capital from several investors. I limited the amount of money that each single investor could contribute so that there would be no "first among equals." I ensured that I would not start with multiple shareholders in a single-voting block attributable to preexisting relationships among them by making sure that my personal relationships with each investor was solid.

I implemented that effort as shareholder diversity, and I remained in charge of my business and in control of my own destiny from the date of formation until the date we sold. Don't create the circumstances under which your shareholders can run you out of your own company by taking the easy way out in raising money from a single investor or a group of related investors. I have seen it happen many times.

When I started Ranchland, my investors owned 80 percent, and I owned 20 percent. They were putting something at risk. I was risking everything and wanted some control of my destiny. Today, that could be accomplished with an LLC, which was not an option in the 1960s. My answer was setting up a Sub-S corporation. I got all voting stock, and the investors got both voting and nonvoting stock in a ratio that gave the entire investor group 55 percent of the vote and I had 45 percent. I explained to them that, whereas they were only putting up money, I was putting my future on the line. However, because I respected them and their business acumen, if they nearly all disagreed with me—they might even be right—then their vote could prevail. The ideal investor can contribute more to your company than just money. Expertise (lawyers, CPAs, etc.), advice, and contacts are a few of the extras your investors will hopefully bring along with their money.

Divide and multiply.

My Ranchland property was half a mile north of Farm to Market Road (FM) 1171 near Roanoke, Texas—a paved, secondary, east-west thoroughfare north of Dallas-Fort Worth. Many visitors experienced difficulty in finding the backroad entrance to the ranch. I wanted Ranchland to have an entrance directly off of FM 1171, so

I went about looking at adjacent properties that did in fact front on FM 1171.

One such property was a one-hundred-acre tract divided by FM 1171 into two parcels, sixty-five acres north of FM 1171 on the same side as Ranchland, and thirty-five acres on the south side of FM 1171. I searched the deed records and eventually found out that the one hundred acres were owned by the twenty-one heirs of the original owner, and that all but one of those heirs lived out of state. The one Texas heir lived only fifteen minutes from the ranch. I called the largest heir who lived in Arizona and learned that he could speak for most of the heirs and would, in fact, be willing to sell for $2,000 an acre; however, because so many heirs were involved, it had to be an all-cash sale. My cash position was approximately zero. The one local heir—I dubbed him "Roanoke Willie"—had been looking after the property for his relatives. I didn't have $200,000 and wasn't even certain that I could borrow $200,000, but I continued to think about that property and the Ranchland access I needed.

One day, I noticed a man with a tractor out working the property. I stopped to talk. It turned out that he was paying Willie to rent the one hundred acres. He was a local farmer whom Roanoke Willie had promised 5 percent of the proceeds of any sale as compensation for the erosion control the farmer had put in place on the property. Because I knew from the primary heir that Roanoke Willie only owned 1 or 2 percent, I was confident that he had no ability or intention to perform on his promise of 5 percent of any sales proceeds. I also quietly determined that the other heirs were unaware of Willie's promise to his tenant. Additionally, Roanoke Willie was not sharing the proceeds of the rent he was collecting. I made these points to the local farmer and offered him $2,500 to release any and all claims he might have if I was able to buy the property. He understood the situation and agreed to the $2,500.

I had previously noticed a large estate adjacent on the east side of the property and on the same side of FM 1171 as Ranchland. The owner, Gary Levitz, was the heir to and the successful-in-his-own-right operator of the Levitz Furniture chain. My banker, Walter, knew Gary and agreed to arrange a lunch meeting to introduce us.

I then developed a plan: Working with the primary heir, I entered into two contracts in the name of Jay D. Rodgers and/or assigns. (Never make an offer on real estate without adding "and/or assigns" to the name of the buyer.) One contract was for the sixty-five acres north of FM 1171 at $2,600-plus an acre, and the second contract was for the thirty-five acres south of FM 1171 at $886-plus an acre. The thirty-five-acre contract had a provision requiring the sixty-five-acre contract to be funded before I could close on the smaller tract. This assured the sellers of receiving their full asking price of $2,000 an acre for the one hundred acres. A couple of days after the two contracts had been signed, I met my banker and Gary for lunch.

At lunch, I told Gary about my two contracts and that trying to close on both would stretch me. I told him that the sixty-five acres immediately to the west of his magnificent estate would be an attractive addition to his holdings. He agreed and asked me what I wanted for that contract. I told him that I wanted a road easement to Ranchland down the far west side of his soon-to-be new holding and a check for $5,000 to assign the sixty-five-acre contract to him. He agreed on the spot, and three weeks later, Gary closed on the sixty-five acres. Gary could, and did, pay cash for that property. I paid the farmer $2,500 out of Gary's $5,000 and gave the banker the remaining $2,500 for setting up the luncheon with Gary.

After my lunch with Gary, I had called two former Kodak customers, told them in detail exactly what I had done, and offered to sell each one-third of the thirty-five-acre tract for $20,000 each. At that point, I had spent over a year on the deal, and land value had been going straight up. The fair market was between $2,500 and $3,000 an acre. They both jumped on my offer. When the dust settled, the ranch had an entrance on FM 1171, I owned one-third of the thirty-five acres free and clear, and I had received over $8,000 in cash at the closing.

Thank goodness I did not limit my thinking to just acquiring an easement. Sometimes it's just better to buy more than what you want in order to end up with what you want.

PS Today, as I write this book in 2022, the land in that area starts at $60,000 an acre.

Put your eggs in one basket.

Diversification is touted as a tried-and-true principle in investment management. That classic portfolio theory suggests that the prudent investor allocates his investable wealth over a diversified array of assets such as stocks, bonds, commodities, precious metals, and real estate. In recent years, the list has expanded to include foreign equities. Diversification is designed to reduce risk; however, I believe it is guaranteed to reduce the size of your win.

You have probably heard the story of the general who sailed to a foreign land with all his troops. After disembarking, the troops looked back to see all three of their ships fully engulfed in flames. The general announced that they were there to conquer or perish.

Just like the general, when you're fully committed and your future depends on it, your odds of winning go up dramatically.

I speak with many young entrepreneurs who would like to start their own businesses but are afraid to leave the supposed security of their current jobs. Their excuse is that they would—if they did not have a spouse and/or children to provide for. Paychecks are addictive and a major barrier on the road to wealth creation. Better to try and fail than die never knowing if your vision would have taken you to the moon.

Fortunately, unlike the general's troops, even if they risk it all and fail, they won't perish. Young entrepreneurs should ignore "don't put all your eggs in one basket." Typically

1. they have a small net worth and very little to lose;
2. most of their assets are bankruptcy proof;
3. they have a lifetime to rebuild; and
4. they have the energy to ensure their family will continue to have a roof over their head and three meals a day.

If you want to win the lottery, you have got to buy a ticket. In my opinion, young entrepreneurs who see an opportunity should put all of their eggs in one basket, focus on that basket, and give it tender loving care.

Now that I'm in my early eighties, I don't pay much attention to conventional wisdom that says I should be financially conservative, invest in bonds, and avoid risks. Prudent? Yes, but being a serial entrepreneur—when I find a deal that I believe will be a major winner—I still occasionally put way too many eggs in one basket.

A good example is Applied DNA Sciences, Inc. Ten years ago, when I first became acquainted with the company, it was an over-the-counter penny stock. I studied the company, watched it closely, and became acquainted with top management; by the time they were listed on the NASDAQ, I had invested just over $1 million in their stock—more than I ever have before or since invested in a company I did not control. Since then, they have experienced many of the trials and tribulations of growing companies. The market value of my investment has ranged from a paper profit of $1 million to a loss of over $600,000. My friends suggested that I not provide the hard numbers in this book. They were afraid that if the company does not do well, I'll look bad. My answer? Facts are facts. Entrepreneurs take calculated risks, and I continue to believe that this company will go to the moon. If I'm wrong, I'm wrong.

Know your stakeholders.

I was approached by an acquaintance, Bennie, who had been employed in the continuous-forms printing business for many years. The company he worked for had recently been acquired, and the buyer's changes were making the company an unpleasant place to work. Bennie told me that he and two others with a different continuous-forms printing company wanted to start a business to compete with their former employers. Their desire was legitimate because they were not bound by a noncompetition covenant.

I told them that in order for me to help them start a company and invest alongside them, they would have to have skin in the game. I defined skin in the game as each of them investing $20,000. Because all three were working men and had presumably saved little of their wages, I believed that the endeavor would end with this threshold requirement. However, I received a call sometime later from Bennie.

He announced that one of them had cashed in his 401(k) and paid the 10 percent penalty to raise his $20,000. Another had sold his house and moved in to an apartment. Finally, Bennie had remarried his ex-wife and convinced her to dedicate the money she had gotten from him in their divorce to the new business venture. They had called my bluff, and I agreed to put up an additional $150,000.

Printing companies are traditionally low-leveraged, capital-intensive businesses. However, we found an equipment manufacturer that had recently repossessed $1.5 million worth of nearly new printing equipment. Because they were highly motivated, we were able to buy it with no money down, no payments for six months, and half payments for the second six months. Additionally, we convinced a large paper supplier to put $250,000 in paper inventory on the floor of our new facility and give us 120-day terms. We, no doubt, set the record for being the most highly leveraged company in the industry.

I wanted Bennie to understand that the risk the paper company was taking was even greater than my $150,000. Enroute to a meeting with our paper supplier one day, I asked Bennie, "Do you know who the biggest stakeholder in our business is?"

Bennie said, "Why, you are, Jay."

At that point, we were pulling in to the paper company's parking lot, and I changed the subject.

Once we arrived at the paper company's CEO's office, I asked him if he knew who the biggest stakeholder in our company was. He responded, "You're damn right I do. I am." My friend Bennie never forgot that lesson.

I am happy to report that all three of the working founders retired as millionaires.

Don't allow short-term benefits to be detrimental to your game-winning homerun. Be the biggest risk-taker in your deals.

There's a disturbing pattern in America today to use other people's money for everything. We see that pattern in Congress, in charities (where, many times, way too much of the money goes to the staff rather than to the charitable purpose for which it was purportedly raised), and—sadly—in entrepreneurship.

I have always taken the position that I owe it to my investors to take the biggest financial risk in every business venture I launch. If I'm using somebody else's money, I want them to know that I'll suffer the biggest loss if we fail, and I want them to be assured that we are equally yoked in the venture and will win or lose together. I take no management or promotional fee and use no other ploy to boost my return at the expense of my investors. It is the alignment of my interests with the interests of my investors that has allowed me to participate alongside the same core group of investors for decades and to continue to count all of them as friends through both wins and losses. For the past forty-eight years, a few phone calls have been all that has been needed to raise money for a new venture.

Once your business is experiencing success, the natural tendency is to increase the amount of your salary—sometimes even to astro-nomical levels. Your paychecks can become extremely expensive when it's time to sell your company; equally expensive is the practice of living off the company. By this I mean running many personal expenses through the company as business expenses: entertainment, travel, personal vehicles, insurance, family employee paychecks, etc. Using the rule of thumb that small private businesses are worth four-to-five times earnings, each dollar you siphon from the company's annual earnings will cost four to five dollars when you sell the company. Yes, recasting plays a role, but dirty books are dirty books.

While it's true that your prospective buyer may attempt to recast the company's earnings to show the business's actual bottom line, the higher you set the compensation bar for the function you perform, the easier it becomes for the buyer to do likewise. Typically, the buyer will have some concerns about how important your role in the company is to its success. Again, the higher the compensation, the more the concern.

If you absolutely must have more money, borrow it from the company at the lowest legal interest rate and pay the loan off with capital gains dollars at the closing table when the business sells. If the personal expenses you have run through the company are well hidden, they won't be recast. If they are not well hidden, the IRS may want to talk to you. The cleaner your books are the last three years prior to sale, the more capital gains dollars you can expect to receive for the company.

As you build your business, make sure that you—not a supplier or a customer—are in charge and in control your destiny.

Many readers will be acquainted with the danger of a small business having one or two customers that represent a significant portion of their revenues and/or profits. Some might pick a slightly higher or lower number, or the nature of the business might encourage a higher or lower number. My rule of thumb is: no customer should represent over 15 percent of your revenues. The danger is that if the customer goes away, much of the fixed overhead that you have taken on to serve that customer will not go away. Bankers are particularly wary of lending to a customer with this problem.

My wife, Bettye, Robert Fielder (a long-time employee and then partner), and I formed Healthcare Staff Resources (HSR) with $3,000 in capital. The mission of HSR was to provide physical therapists, occupational therapists, and pharmacists to healthcare facilities. In north Texas, there is perhaps no bigger health care provider than Parkland Memorial Hospital. As Dallas County's public hospital, Parkland sees more patients each year than any of its privately owned competitors. We at HSR were, therefore, overjoyed when Parkland contracted with us to provide physical therapists and occupational therapists to Parkland. HSR began to grow rapidly as Parkland ordered more and more coverage. At a monthly board meeting, I learned that, almost overnight, Parkland had become our largest customer and accounted for over 40 percent of our revenue. As chairman, I was able to get agreement on and institute a policy that forbade the company from allowing a customer to represent over 15 percent of our revenues. Additionally, we agreed that—even at the risk of losing the Parkland account—within forty-five days, we would be in compliance with our new policy. We were still small enough and growing fast enough that these policies would not inflict a mortal wound.

We did lose the Parkland account. I'm happy to report, however, that less than sixty days after we lost it, Parkland announced that they would no longer be working with outside PT and OT staffing firms and that all funds for this staffing had been cut off.

As I mentioned earlier, having too much revenue concentrated among one or two customers is dangerous. Equally dangerous, but less commonly discussed, is the danger of a small business having only one source of supply for any unique or critical item. When we started Smart Start, we knew on day one that to build a meaningful business and control our own destiny, we would have to have our own ignition interlock device. The fact is that it took a great deal longer than we originally anticipated, but we were able to build our own device and had an outside firm manufacture per our specifications.

As chairman for over a year, I encouraged the CEO to seek a second source for the manufacture of our device. At that point, I gave him a very-easy-to-understand ultimatum regarding a second source for our device. Five months later, the second source was producing a few devices for us. Thirty days after that, totally unaware that we even had a second source, our original manufacturer informed us that they were restructuring their company and product line, effective immediately, and would no longer be able to supply us. It had taken almost six months to get our second source up to speed, but they were able to take over without causing a supply problem.

Six months without units would have been disastrous to our growing business. Needless to say, we immediately set about establishing another second source.

—5—

Motivations

One of the best traits of successful entrepreneurs is the ability to judge people and their motivations and to understand what makes them tick.

If you can see John Jones through John Jones's eyes, you can sell John Jones what John Jones buys.

During my Ranchland days, I spent a considerable amount of money on direct mail. I used direct mail pieces to attract both youngsters to my summer youth ranch program and corporations for my corporate dude ranch and meeting facilities. The closest post office to Ranchland was fifteen minutes away in the rural community of Roanoke, Texas. The post office building occupied less than one thousand square feet. At that time in the late 1960s, the number of stamps a post office sold was a key factor in its rating.

The magnitude of my direct mail operation had a major impact on the little post office in Roanoke. Because of our stamp purchases, the Roanoke post office was allowed to install a telephone which had not previously been permitted. Additionally, all the employees—except the postmaster—received a raise.

I remembered this lesson a few years later when I signed on to help American Health Profiles (AHP), working with Farmland Industries and their many midwestern rural cooperatives to provide mobile multiphasic health testing to their members. We sent out hundreds of thousands of direct mail pieces promoting the service, and timing was critical to coordinate the mailing with the arrival of the mobile health vans. Because I understood the post office's rating system, I was always able to motivate a postmaster to go above and beyond.

AHP could never receive discounted postage or any other sort of financial remuneration for directing its business to a particular post office, nor could we offer additional compensation for accommodating our frequently time-pressured schedule. However, the local postmasters who would stay open late for us and would open the back door for us on Saturday or Sunday (if need be) were the ones who got our stamp business and mailing volume. It was a great negotiating tool. My understanding is that the stamp sales revenues today are no longer considered in post office ratings, but the volume of mail is.

Do your research and understand what motivates someone.

In the process of selling our healthcare staffing business, I spent significant time identifying prospective buyers for our company. One of those prospects, Hooper Holmes, initially stood out from the rest. I succeeded in securing an audience with a decision maker, and a visit was arranged for an executive of the company to evaluate our business and report on how suitable our company was for acquisition by Hooper Holmes.

I spent my time telling her what a great, clean, well-run company we were selling. I showed her our business in detail, including our financial statements, introductions to key operating personnel, and references from well-known customers. She listened and observed intently. Our company was a perfect addition to their core business.

Upon her departure, I was convinced that I had landed our buyer. I was surprised a few days later to receive a communication that Hooper Holmes would not be proceeding with the acquisition of our business. Believing that Hooper had been the perfect prospect, even though the opportunity had been lost, I did some digging—due diligence that I should have done prior to her arrival, not after.

It turned out that the VP who had visited to assess our business had originally been a registered nurse (RN) in a management position with Hooper Holmes. A few years earlier, she had brought an acquisition opportunity to the company's attention. They acquired the company and, because it was in her area of expertise, put her in charge of that acquisition. In only two years, she had doubled revenues, tripled profits, and was rewarded with a promotion to VP and a major raise.

This information was readily available; in fact, she had mentioned the prior acquisition while she was there touring my company. If I had listened to her as carefully as she had listened to me, I would have realized that she was interested in buying a business that offered an opportunity for her to shine. She was looking for a repeat of her earlier success. I had convinced her that we had a smooth, well-run business with little room for improvement. Had I done my homework and understood her perspective, I would have spent my time talking about the opportunities we had not bothered to pursue and the mistakes we had made. My presentation had, unfortunately, been very effective. I convinced her that our company offered her little opportunity for another overnight success story.

To this day, I believe Hooper Holmes should have bought our company, but I've never forgotten the painful lesson I learned. I now do my due diligence before, not after, the presentation. I focus on what the buyer wants to buy, not what I am trying to sell. That means I ask a lot of questions, listen closely to the answers, and put my ego and pride aside.

— 6 —

Learn from Your Mistakes and Failures

The wise man uses mistakes to fuel his future, while the fool looks at a mistake as a failure. Mistakes are a part of life, and the sooner you realize that and glean some valuable lessons from them, the better off you'll be.

There is a lot to be said for learning from our mistakes.

When I was in my late twenties or early thirties, I decided to get my pilot's license. I went to the FBO at the Denton Airport in Texas and signed up for lessons. While I was there, I met another enrolling student named George. After talking for a while, George and I decided to team up and take our lessons back-to-back so that, when George took his lesson, I could sit behind George and our instructor Bill, and listen and learn. When it was my turn, we would simply switch places. This plan worked out great, and we also studied together for our ground school tests.

A few weeks in to this arrangement, I arrived for our lessons; Bill told me that George had called to say that a family situation had come up and he would not be joining us today. Bill and I preflighted the plane and flew out west of Denton. When we returned to the airport, our normal routine was to do a few touch-and-goes. As I was on final approach, Bill said, "When you land, just pull over on the taxiway and stop."

When I stopped, Bill informed me that he was getting out and that I was going to solo. I was absolutely astounded.

"What do you mean?" I said. "How can I solo? George hasn't soloed yet, and he makes great landings every time."

His response was, "Jay, you have screwed up nearly every landing and made every mistake known to mankind. You have mastered correcting and recovering. I know that if something goes wrong, you will be able to right it and land safely. Because George always lands perfectly, I have no idea what he will do when he has a problem. Until I do, he is not ready to solo."

My instructor's thinking highlights the value of mentors and coaches. People who have the experience, who "have been there and done that," often see the road ahead more clearly than those of us who are traveling it for the first time.

Mistakes are a part of life.
Admit them, address them, and move on.

I have always believed that when you have a problem in business, the quicker you face up to it and address it, the better off you are. Ideally, you will contact your affected customers before the problem and consequences come to their attention. Explain the problem. Take responsibility for the problem. Explain to them the plan you have put in place to correct the issue. Give them a timetable for solving the issue, and take whatever steps are necessary to retain them as loyal customers.

Unfortunately, in some cases, you aren't made aware of the problem until it's too late to follow the course of action outlined above. Such was the case with a mistake we made in the late 1980s when we were in the business of staffing healthcare professionals. At this stage in my life, I can look back on the incident and laugh; however, let me assure you that it wasn't funny at the time.

A large hospital, located just a few miles from our offices, retained us to identify and recruit a new director for their pharmacy. We found the perfect individual. The hospital administrator was ecstatic and hired the man with the agreement that he would start in forty-five days. With our task accomplished, our billing department sent the hospital an invoice for the agreed upon fee of $25,000.

Two days later while we were sitting around patting ourselves on the back for a job well done, I received a call from the hospital administrator. The words "livid" and "irate" grossly understate the administrator's frame of mind when I answered his call.

The administrator, as it turned out, had not yet informed his current pharmacy director that he was being replaced. He had planned to wait until the date for his new hire's arrival was closer. Unfortunately, our billing department had made it a moot issue. Rather than sending our invoice directly to the hospital administrator, they sent it to the hospital's pharmacy director. The pharmacy director, seeing the invoice and realizing that he was being replaced, had just walked into the administrator's office with our invoice in hand and asked the administrator if there was something he needed to know.

Needless to say, it was not our finest hour.

When you make a mistake, handle it and move on.

Because we provided staffing services to hospitals and other healthcare providers, many assumed that a lengthy collections cycle was the inevitable result of the business niche we had chosen to enter; I was unwilling to accept that assessment. When our A/R aging got totally out of hand, I announced at a company meeting that we would reduce our collections cycle to twenty days for all privately owned healthcare facilities we served and forty-five days for all government facilities. Helen, our CFO, promptly announced that this goal could not be achieved. My response: "We're going to do it, and we're sure going to miss you." I promptly assigned collections as the number one priority of one of our employees.

A good collections person must be temperamentally suited to the task. The task requires persistence, a thick skin, a pleasant demeanor, and the assertiveness to politely call the customer to account when it turns out that the check really wasn't in the mail. Our collections cycle was reduced to fewer than twenty days (eighteen, to be precise) for our privately owned customer and to forty-five days for our government accounts. Although it's incorrect to assert that nothing is impossible, most things are possible. We don't ever know what's actually possible until we fully commit to achieving the goal. You have to do what it takes until it works. That was the approach we used with our clients. We told them that although we were the world's best medical staffing company, we were not prepared to be their bankers.

The value of proper policies and procedures was proven again when we sold Healthcare Staff Resources to Kimberly Quality Care, a division of the New York Stock Exchange company Lifetime. Their President, Larry Stusser, was concerned that we had receivables of nearly $500,000 on the books and had only a $5,000 allowance for bad debt. Rather than rewrite the definitive agreement, we resolved the issue by shaking hands on a gentlemen's agreement that, 120 days after the closing, I would send Larry a check for all receivables on the books at closing exceeding $5,000 that had not been collected. In turn, he would send me a check for any of the $5,000 that had not been needed to cover uncollected receivables on the books at closing. Less than ninety days after the closing, I received his check in the amount of $5,000.

Incidentally, Helen got on board with our collections goal, remained as the company's CFO, and performed admirably all the way through our selling of the company. In addition to her company bonus at sale, I rewarded her with five thousand shares of stock in our next venture, which I started two years later. The company recently sold, and her five thousand shares got her a $1 million check.

Despite the fact that most things "can be done," if you believe it can't . . . you'll be right.

Always look for the gems that hide in the rubble.

If you've ever failed, as most of us have, you've learned quite a few lessons.

While attending Harvard's Owner/President Management (OPM) Program in the early 1990s, I developed what has proven to be a lifelong, close friendship with Ruth Freiman, a fellow classmate who resided in Ottawa, Canada. Over lunch one day, I casually mentioned that I had always wanted to attend the Calgary Stampede. Having briefly rodeoed and ridden saddle broncos and bareback horses in my younger days (not very successfully), I was well aware that it was considered the world's best rodeo. Ruth responded, "Then why the heck don't you?" She went on to mention that she and her husband were good friends of Bill Pratt, who had been the general manager of

71

the rodeo for many years. Ruth contacted Bill and the result was that, in 1999, Bill arranged for Bettye and me to be invited as VIP guests of the Calgary Stampede. The die was cast, and prior to the pandemic, we enjoyed twenty consecutive summer trips to Calgary. Bettye and I quickly got into the habit of arriving a couple of weeks before the stampede and making up for that by staying a couple of weeks after it ended. We even bought a condo for use during our summer visits.

Over the years, Bettye and I developed relationships with the officers and directors of the stampede, and these friendships became the primary reason we continue to spend summers there. The stampede is quite a spectacle, and one of the most exciting events is the chuck wagon races. I call the event "The NASCAR of the North": thirty-six drivers, four horse teams, and chuck wagons participate in heats of four—nine races each of the ten nights. In addition to the nightly prize, the top winner for the ten performances receives $100,000. Because corporations compete to sponsor the chuck wagons, the stampede created an auction, whereby prospective sponsors could bid for the right to provide the chuck wagon tarp complete with the corporate logo for their driver. It's not unusual for the winning bid for the best driver's wagon to top $150,000. The stampede divides the take between the driver and the stampede.

After noting many similarities and common interests that first trip between my friends in Calgary and my friends in Texas (energy and ranching being two of the biggest), I decided that next year I would put together a consortium of Texas sponsors for a chuck wagon with a tarp, styled with "Texas Friends of the Calgary Stampede." The tarp would feature a different Texas-sponsoring company each of the ten nights. I didn't consider the challenge of raising $200,000 for the auction and funding ten nights of social events at the Wagon Barn to be difficult. Many of the companies I had decided to approach were Texas-based companies already doing a lot of business in Calgary. I personally put up a $10,000 deposit with Jason Glass, a past champion driver in the chuck wagon races. When I returned to Texas after that summer, I resolved to get introduced into the Houston oil and gas community, which I felt represented the biggest pool of my prospective Texas sponsors.

I called my Houston attorney-friend Gary Trichter and scheduled a meeting. At the last minute, Gary was called out of town, but recruited his friend Carolyn Faulk to meet with us. Carolyn is the successful owner and operator of a Houston-based plastics distribution business and is also a director of the Houston Livestock Show and Rodeo (HLSR). Carolyn listened attentively to my plan and invited us to dinner that evening to discuss it further. Because it was Bettye's and my anniversary, I declined by telling Carolyn that we already had anniversary reservations at Café Annie's, an exclusive Houston restaurant, which is now known as RDG. After Bettye and I had been seated there that evening, the waiter delivered a bottle of Dom Perignon to the table and announced that it was courtesy of Carolyn. When it came time for us to leave and I asked for the check, the waiter announced that the check had also been taken care of courtesy of Carolyn—an incredibly gracious gesture by someone we had just met.

Over time, Carolyn introduced us to numerous directors of the HLSR and to many of its officers. They, in turn, introduced us to executives at several of the Texas companies doing business in Calgary, which I had targeted as potential sponsors of our chuck wagon. I had gone so far as to engage an artist to do a colorful contemporary painting of a racing chuck wagon.

I used the artwork both in my presentations to the sponsors and on T-shirts. Unfortunately, my best efforts to enlist sponsors and raise the funds were less than successful. I only received pledges for about half of the funds needed and ended up releasing those. Although less-than-successful is kinder and gentler, the fact is that my efforts failed. I threw in the towel when I finally realized that I had not properly analyzed the project. The lesson I learned was that Texas companies doing business in Calgary wanted to pass themselves off as companies with roots in the Calgary community and did not want to attract attention as interlopers. They worked hard to fly under the radar and be successful while maintaining a low profile.

When forced to acknowledge my failure, I engaged an artist to paint a picture in morbid colors of a chuck wagon being driven over a cliff. I presented both artist renderings the next summer at a Calgary party we hosted for our friends there and where I was compelled to concede defeat. That painting still hangs in my office to remind me of the experience and the lessons I learned.

But all was not lost. My newfound friends at the Houston Livestock Show and Rodeo invited me to participate with the Valley Lodge Trail Riders Association that rides in to Houston each year to open the HLSR. My participation led to an invitation to be a guest of the board for the annual week-long ride in South Texas with the Tejas Vaqueros—a great group of 350 horsemen, of which I am now a full-fledged member. Other contacts arranged for me to ride as a guest of the board with the thousand-member riding group near Santa Barbara, California: a great organization called Los Rancheros Visitadores, which Ronald Reagan was a member of. Carolyn Faulk and a couple of her friends have joined a group that Bettye and I cruise with annually, and they are outstanding additions to our crowd.

The chuck wagon tarp experience was definitely one of my most successful and rewarding failures.

— 7 —

Plans and Predictions

I have always enjoyed playing poker. In my early thirties, I got serious about it for a period of time. Although gambling is technically illegal in Texas, there are several regular poker games that take place. Because both my brother-in-law and a close personal friend owned construction companies, I started playing regularly with a group of contractors. Routinely, their crews got under way by 7:00 a.m. and they had been up for a couple of hours by then. On game nights, they would rush home after shutting down the crews for the day, grab a quick shower, inhale some dinner, and head to the game. Because it was their night out, they would invariably overindulge in "authority water" while enjoying the comradery.

I, on the other hand, was focused totally on winning. Many of the pots would contain over $500, and pots in excess of $1,000 were not rare. I wasn't then, and have never been, among the world's great poker players, but thanks to numerous strategic advantages, I was a very consistent winner. On game days, I slept late, ate moderately, had an hour or an hour-and-a-half massage, and finished my pregame midafternoon meal a couple of hours before game time. I drank almost nothing prior to and during the game. All in all, those practices gave me a huge advantage at the table.

In applying my belief that if you wanted to win, it was important that you not play with people who were better than you. I kept extremely accurate records of each player's winnings and losses. This allowed me to frequently avoid getting in an expensive heads-up situation with the one contractor who consistently won.

I convinced myself that—even though I was perhaps not too far above average as a poker player—with proper preparation, discipline, and procedures, I could consistently win. And with only one or two games a week, I could make a living. Despite that, I stopped playing regularly and for the last forty-plus years have played very rarely.

The two major factors in deciding to give up playing regularly were these:

1. By applying the same amount of time and energy, business and investment opportunities were much more rewarding and frequently more fun.

2. When I analyzed it, I realized that all the combined time and energy expended by all the players in the game did not produce or create anything. They simply redistributed existing wealth. Therefore, you could only feel good about it if you accepted the fact that it had some recreational value.

Be specific with your plan. Many brilliant entrepreneurs have failed without a clear plan. It's awfully hard to get there if you don't know where you're going.

Three years after my wife, Bettye, and I formed our healthcare staffing company, we set the date for selling the company an additional three years out and circled it on the calendar: June 30, 1990. I believed that having audited financial statements would be a great advantage in selling our company, so over three years before our targeted sales date I engaged Deloitte Haskins & Sells (now just Deloitte) to annually audit the books of our company. I have never been completely convinced that professional fees bear much relationship to the time actually spent, even though attorneys and CPAs all purport to and may well bill by the hour. Because I thought that Deloitte would charge more and more each year as they saw that I was growing and getting closer and closer to selling the company, I insisted on a three-year bid for the three years of audited financials I would need before our anticipated sale. I told them we would grow at least 400 percent over the next three years. Deloitte initially resisted, but finally relented and gave me the three-year quote I had asked for.

We missed our targeted sale date by forty-five days. However, because we sold to a public company, the buyer insisted that we engage Deloitte to provide an audit opinion covering the last forty-five days we owned the business. Deloitte's bill to us for the forty-five-day stub period exceeded the entire amount we paid them for the preceding fiscal year. Upon receipt of Deloitte's bill, I could only laugh.

Draw your own conclusions, and plan and negotiate accordingly.

When we put Healthcare Staff Resources up for sale, Brad Hummel, the CEO of Diagnostic Health Services, called and made an appointment to come out and see the company. He brought his CPA, Frank Adams, with him. I was so impressed with Frank and told him at the first meeting that, if his client bought our company, he could handle the closing numbers for both sides. Ultimately Brad's board of directors refused to approve his purchasing our company. Despite not selling him the company, two outstanding things happened:

The first was that I developed my relationship with Frank Adams and later hired him as CEO of Physician Staffing Resources with the assignment of selling that company. When he sold the company, he stayed aboard with the new owners and later when they sold, he stayed on with the buyers again. As a result, I am able to add him to the long list of entrepreneurs that I have played a significant role in making multimillionaires. Additionally, we have done several other deals together and remain close friends.

The second great thing that happened was that Brad was nice enough to suggest that I should contact Kimberly Quality Care, a division of the New York Stock Exchange company, Lifetime, as they were looking to acquire companies like mine. Brad gave me the name and number of Larry Stusser, the CEO of Kimberly Quality Care. During the conversation Larry asked me how we handled our care-givers, meaning did we treat them as employees or as contract labor that received a 1099-S. At that time, the IRS had a major campaign underway to penalize and convert companies that inappropriately handle employees as contract labor. I told Larry that we handled our caregivers as contract labor.

He then asked, "Jay, how do you feel about that?"

I said, "Larry, it scares the hell out of me."

The truth is amazingly powerful. The definitive agreement we signed left us liable for any fines or penalties the IRS imposed prior to the date of sale. Several months after the sale, we had a meeting with Larry's people as well as lawyers, CPAs, and the IRS; there must've been eight or ten of us. Larry negotiated an agreement with the IRS to convert all of the caregivers to employees with the understanding that there would be no retroactive fines or penalties. Invariably, you'll make better deals when you deal with smart people and shoot straight. Just for the record, when the sale funded, I sent a check for $5,000 made out personally to Brad Hummel.

Don't forget to say thank you.

Don't predict. Protect.

While our preference for selling Healthcare Staff Resources was for an all-cash deal, Larry had proposed using stock as a small part of the consideration for the purchase. We had researched the stock of the parent company, Lifetime Corporation (NYSE), and had found its pricing to be highly stable, hovering at around thirty-five dollars per share and with a long-term uptrend. When Larry repeated his desire to use its stock as partial consideration, I countered with the position that we would accept, provided that the shares were registered and, therefore, freely transferable at issuance. In the days before shelf registrations enabled public companies to issue registered shares at a moment's notice, my request was met with the comment that it would take some weeks to register and deliver those shares to us. My response: provide for additional cash compensation equal to the reduction in value if the share price declines between closing and the delivery of registered, tradeable shares to us.

David advised that I was jeopardizing the transaction over an issue of little impact given the stability of the shares. When the meeting ended, both sides instructed our respective counsel to continue to work on the definitive agreement pending resolution of this remaining issue. Larry ultimately relented, and the counsel included a provision that if the value of the shares declined before they were registered and tradeable, I would receive additional compensation in the amount of the loss in market value of my shares.

We closed on this multimillion-dollar transaction on August 10, 1990. Before the stock was tradeable, the United States initiated Operation Desert Storm and the stock market dropped precipitously. The additional dollars we received definitely had more than "a little impact" on the deal. The price per share later returned to its preinvasion level. We materially enhanced the value of the transaction to our shareholders solely because I refused to accept the past and the present as the predictor of the future.

— 8 —

Know Your Value

Over the years, I've been the principal player in numerous entrepreneurial companies that, in total, have employed thousands of people. In all of these companies, we've made it clear that if any employee was capable of handling a better job than we could provide, we would help him or her get it outside of our company.

Dollars are only a small part of compensation.

In keeping with that philosophy and commitment, Mark was a young man who had originally been a counselor in our summer youth ranch program and was then promoted. He had been an equally outstanding youth ranch program director the summer prior to and following his graduation from college. When the summer ended, he wanted to stay on at the ranch, but we didn't have an opening deserving of his capabilities. For his benefit, I insisted that he focus on advancing his career. A few days later, I was invited by a neighbor to a party and was introduced to a friend of theirs visiting from Tennessee. The friend, Rhett Ball, was a fine southern gentleman and the President/CEO of American Health Profiles. At that time, the company provided mobile, multiphase health testing to the members of various unions. I arranged for him to meet and interview Mark.

Mark was immediately offered a job and, shortly thereafter, moved to Tennessee to join American Health Profiles.

A few months later, I decided to take a year off and leased the ranch. I had stayed in touch with Mark, and he shared with Mr. Ball my intention to take a sabbatical. Mr. Ball picked up the phone and, in his soft-talking southern style, convinced me to fly to Nashville and discuss a project they were about to begin. When I arrived, he told me they were in the final stages of discussions with the world's largest agriculture co-op, Farmland Industries, to provide mobile multiphase health testing to the rural community members of their nearly two thousand local co-ops located throughout the Midwest. He knew from our original meeting that I had rural Midwest agricultural background and wanted me to head up opening this new market.

Value first. Compensation second.

The fact that I was trying to avoid work, not find it, and was used to being my own boss put me in a very strong position when we did negotiate my joining the project. As the great negotiator Herb Cohen always preached when negotiating, "Care, but not too much." I finally agreed to come aboard for six months to launch the project.

At that point, Mr. Ball asked me what I thought I should receive in compensation. Aware that the company had in excess of one hundred employees, I told him that neither he nor I had any idea what I was worth in that position. However, if I were to join the effort, I had two requirements: First, an understanding that the company founder and Mr. Ball would obviously both be better paid than me. I wanted to be the third best-paid person in the company and initially didn't care if it was only by a dollar. I felt that if they weren't willing to bring me in at that level, I was not interested in postponing my sabbatical to be part of the project. Second, after ninety days, I wanted to sit down with Mr. Ball. At that time, with a little experience behind us, we could decide what I was worth.

Mr. Ball agreed. Ninety days later, we were at Farmland Industries' headquarters in Kansas City, Missouri, staying at the then newly opened Crown Center. Mr. Ball invited me to his suite and, reminding me that my ninety days were up, wanted to know what I now felt I was worth. I told him that I had written the exact dollar figure on a piece of paper that was in my shirt pocket, but I added that I felt that it was much more important to know what he felt I was worth. His offer was a mammoth increase. At that point, I removed and unfolded the paper in my pocket. It was identical to the offer he had just made.

That soft-talking southern gentleman managed to keep me onboard for almost two years. It was the only salaried job I ever held after leaving Kodak, and it was a fascinating and rewarding experience. I was offered Mr. Ball's job when he announced that he was going to retire. I had, however, already stayed longer than planned and was overdue to reenter my own entrepreneurial world.

The biggest bonus from my time with American Health Profiles was meeting their vice president, Bettye Akin. We married eight years later. Another plus was that Mr. Ball convinced me to attend Harvard's OPM entrepreneurial program. The program is a total of nine weeks, three weeks each year for three years. The experience enhanced and expanded my business and personal life in many wonderful ways. I highly recommend it.

Your time is valuable. Don't be afraid to disrupt an industry's current process in favor of a better one. This philosophy applies to every industry.

When we started Physician Staffing Resources, we originally assisted hospital administrators in making certain that their emergency rooms had an adequate number of properly trained and credentialed emergency physicians.

I had assembled and represented the investor group, and I was, as always, the single largest investor. Although I was not personally involved on a daily basis, I felt a responsibility to the investors I had encouraged to participate.

My partner was doing a great job of managing the contracts we had, and each contract produced a good gross profit; however, we needed more contracts to be bottom-line profitable. Looking at the financial statements, I could see that our sales expense was exorbitant—airfare, hotels, and entertainment. Added to that was the time required to travel to hospitals nationally, assess the needs of the potential client, and prepare a proposal. We were only closing a deal for about one-in-six trips.

I believed that many of the requests for proposals came from administrators who had already decided on another provider or course of action but just wanted our proposal as a bargaining tool. We studied and discussed the problem at length and came up with what proved to be an outstanding solution.

We responded to all future RFPs by saying we were unwilling to reply to any RFP without thoroughly evaluating the needs of the hospital and the community. This typically took one or two days on site, and the charge was $2,500 per day plus expenses. We added that if the potential client did not find our evaluation report to be worth more than they paid for it, we would not submit a bill. (No hospital ever asked to not be billed.)

We assured our potential clients that the report would be extremely helpful whether they hired us or another provider. In the event that we were the successful bidder, the cost of the evaluation would be credited back on future invoices.

From the day we began the program and its policies, we made far fewer sales trips, our close rate soared, and we became profitable.

Build a legacy and a business based on integrity.

Silver, like most commodities, fluctuates in value over time. At no time in my life did silver fluctuate more in value than in the early 1980s. The best-known reason for the fluctuation in value then was the attempt by Herbert, Bunker, and Lamar Hunt to corner the silver market. Sons of the famed oil wildcatter H.L. Hunt and billionaires themselves individually, the Hunt brothers knew quite a lot about commodities. The more silver they acquired and controlled, the higher the price of silver went. My work with photo finishers and X-ray film at Kodak had made me very knowledgeable regarding recovering silver from film and photo processing.

It was in this environment that I was dedicating time to acquiring and reselling silver-laden X-ray film. I had an opportunity to buy several thousand pounds of silver-laden X-ray film from a Nashville firm. Before going to Nashville to take the delivery, I made some calls, located a refinery in the hills of Tennessee about sixty miles out of Nashville, and made a firm deal to sell him the film. The price we agreed on would, after all my expenses, give me a net profit of about

$20,000. Because of the activities of the Hunt Brothers, the price of silver had increased substantially by the time I arrived in Nashville. I pointed this fact out to my buyer and demanded a higher price than we had agreed on. He rightly refused, and my greed left me without a buyer.

I spent the next several days in Nashville trying to sell the silver-laden X-ray film, which I was paying a security firm to guard. In the process, I ran up a $600 phone bill and a significant hotel bill. On the fourth day, the price of silver had moved up a little more but was becoming a bit erratic. At that point, I admitted to myself that, in trying to re-trade the deal, I had abandoned my ethics and been a greedy jerk. With that self-confession behind me, I did the only smart thing I had done in the entire process: I swallowed my pride, called my original buyer, admitted to having been out of line, and offered to honor our original agreement. My buyer refused, but countered with an offer a little less than we had originally agreed upon. I replied, "I had that coming; I accept."

I was paid and delivered the silver-laden film early in the afternoon on March 27, 1980, the day known as Silver Thursday.

Before the commodity markets closed that afternoon, silver crashed, falling to $10.80. Before the crash, silver had reached an all-time high of $49.45. Had the sale not been completed before the crash, my net worth would have suffered a major blow. Additionally, I would have been left owing the bank the $100,000 I had borrowed to finance the purchase.

As I flew home, I promised myself that, going forward, my word and my business ethics would always be more important than profit.

A couple of sidelines to my story of silver and greed: When I arrived in Nashville to purchase the X-ray film, after examining the film, I called my bank to fund the loan I had arranged. As it happened, my banker, Walter, was out of the bank when I called, so I left the instructions with his secretary to have him fund the X-ray film loan. By the time Walter got back to the bank, every young lady in the bank had been told, "That Jay Rodgers is over in Tennessee buying X-rated films."

When I made the deal to purchase the X-ray film, I was smoking four packs of Camels a day. By the end of the third day in Nashville, I was up to five packs a day. At this point, I had not thought of calling—let alone mustered up the courage to call—the original refinery back, and panic was setting in. That night I told God that if He would get me out of this mess, I would go home and quit smoking. (Yeah, like I was doing him a favor.)

Deserved or not, He gave me a double win. I survived financially, and at eighty-two, I'm alive and in good health. I smoked my last cigarette on April 4, 1980.

Do what you say and say what you mean. In the business world, lawyers have, unfortunately, replaced handshakes. I believe the very best contract is one that clearly and simply expresses all parties' intents, is signed, and then put in a filing cabinet never to be retrieved.

— 9 —

The Secret Sauce of Sales

When I opened our ranch for corporate business, most of the corporations either used our facility for convention outings or company picnics. Invariably, they would send a handful of the decision-makers for corporate-outing events or the annual company-picnic committee to visit and look us over. I very rapidly perfected my presentation that provided an extremely high close rate when they visited. We toured the ranch, discussed hors d'oeuvres, the complete ranch barbecue menu, arena events, trail riding, and all the other options we could provide. We jointly put together a proposal for the event, and then I gave them a turnkey price for their outing. Typically at that point, they wanted to cut out some of our activities and services to negotiate a lower price.

My response was that we had developed a proposal that they all knew would provide an outstanding afternoon or evening for their customers being bused out from a Dallas or Fort Worth convention or their employees attending the annual picnic with their families. I simply said that only those sitting in the office with me at that time would ever know the cost of the event. However, all their attending customers and/or employees would leave knowing only that it had or had not been an outstanding outing provided by the company. Because of that, and the fact that the reputation of our ranch was of paramount importance to me, I was not willing to agree to host an outing that might be less than outstanding; therefore, at the risk of their not selecting our ranch for their event, I had to stand by the proposal we had prepared.

Selling a product or business doesn't have to be about addressing needs. People make decisions based on desire. Sell to what people want, and you'll always win.

Statistical organizations like Standard & Poor's (S&P) who track business will divide business into numerous categories. One of those categories is consumer discretionary. Early in my business career, I encountered a small, hundred-year-old company that made hand-made, made-to-measure, custom cowboy boots. The company produced magnificent work and could turn out ten to twelve pairs of boots a day but wasn't getting enough orders to keep them busy. I believed that the company should be overrun with orders, and I set out to prove it. Having just wrapped up a major project, I was ready to take on a project that had having fun as its number one goal. The boot venture struck me as the perfect venue.

I engaged a travel-trailer manufacturer to customize one of their small trailers. The door to the back third of the trailer opened to an aisle with shelving on both sides. These shelves were filled with sample boots. The front of the trailer was a small but well-appointed, comfortable living room/showroom.

I enticed a very bright and personable young lady, Katie Barclay, who had worked for me at American Health Profiles, to sign on for the venture. While I oversaw the customizing of the trailer and developed our marketing plan, Katie spent several weeks at the bootmaker's shop learning how to measure to ensure properly fitting boots and learning the construction details and the benefits of our product.

With everything ready and full of enthusiasm, we loaded up, hitched up, and headed out of the DFW Metroplex for West Texas. We went to small ranch communities like Dimmit, Muleshoe, and Hereford. Between getting acquainted with the local motel manager/owner, locating the local café where the ranchers met for coffee and breakfast, and using reciprocity privileges at local country clubs, we could identify most of the top prospects in the county for high-dollar, handmade, made-to-measure boots within thirty-six hours.

We were a bit of a novelty (a dog and pony show come to town), and the word spread quickly. Additionally, we had a very long phone cord that we connected in one of our motel rooms and ran out to the trailer so we could make calls while waiting for appointments or drop-ins. We were definitely pre-cellphone.

Enough interesting happenings took place on this adventure to fill this book. However, a few stand out in my memory:

1. Katie was measuring the president of a small-town bank southwest of Amarillo, and he and I were talking about the local economy. There were a lot of feedlots in the area, and locals still talked about the cattle market taking a dive a few years earlier (they called it "the wreck"). When the subject came up, the banker looked at me and deadly serious said, "Jay, I never knew I was a millionaire until I lost over a million dollars in the wreck and was able to avoid taking bankruptcy."

2. The fact that we were operating in the consumer–discretionary market was made clear to me one day when I overheard

Katie's discussion with a prospective customer. This West Texas rancher said, "Little lady, I don't need no cowboy boots. I have thirty-six pairs of cowboy boots." Katie responded, "Sir, we're not discussing 'need.' " She sold him a pair of white ostrich boots.

3.   While we were back in the Dallas-Fort Worth area celebrating our highly successful West Texas trip, we met a man who sold high-end, custom-made suits to top executives in Dallas, Fort Worth, Oklahoma City, and Tulsa. He took his samples to their offices, measured them, and wrote up their orders at their place of work. We quickly put a two-way referral agreement in place, and overnight, we started calling on oilmen, bankers, lawyers, doctors, and corporate executives at their offices. Because of his referrals to us, our first trip to Tulsa was unbelievably successful.

Make sure your business includes having fun.

In those days, many of the top country and western stars were represented by an agency located—not in Nashville, as one might expect—but in Tulsa, Oklahoma. I sent Larry, our newly hired second salesman, up to call on them, and Katie went along to observe our new man in action. In one day working the agents, Larry sold each of them at least one pair of boots, and some bought two or three pairs.

Only the agency owner had not ordered or shown any interest. Near day's end, Larry walked into the owner's palatial office unannounced and said, "Sir, I have to know! Why haven't you ordered a single pair of our fine boots?"

The boss looked up from behind his massive walnut desk and replied, "I bought a pair of custom-made high dollar boots a few years ago, and they leaked."

Larry opened his sample case, pulled out the highest dollar sample he had, walked over to the boss's wet bar, filled the boot with water, walked back, and set it on the man's fancy desk. Larry then engaged him in a sports conversation they had started in the coffee room earlier. The man visited but never took his eyes off of the boot. About fifteen minutes later, Larry picked up the boot, returned to the wet bar, and poured the water down the drain. With that, he said, "If you will slip off your shoes, Katie can measure you while we select the leather and design your boots. I would recommend ostrich for your first pair. Which of these colors do you prefer?"

Larry played things close to the vest and, had Katie not gone along, I never would have heard this story.

At one point, we were lost on a back road and flagged down a mud-covered pickup driven by a man I figured for a ranch hand. He was so accommodating that I suggested he come by our trailer for coffee when he was in town. He did and bought one pair of the least expensive (never say cheapest) boots we sold.

While our new friend the ranch hand, Carl Brugal, was being measured, he asked if we had ever taken our boot trailer to Amarillo, Texas, about forty-five miles northeast of Hereford, Texas, where we were located that morning.

I said no, and I explained that while we were good at quickly getting acquainted and identifying prospects in the small communities, Amarillo was just too big of a market for us to tackle.

Carl said he had to be in Amarillo later in the week and would meet us and make some introductions. Since he had purchased the least expensive pair of boots we sold and Amarillo was so big, I wasn't much impressed with our chances of selling many boots. However, from day one, we had placed a priority on having fun in the boot business, and Carl was an enjoyable fellow. Carl said he had a meeting at his bank on Thursday that would be over about 10:00 a.m., so Katie Barclay and I agreed to meet him at the bank then. We arrived a few minutes early and, while sitting in the lobby, I picked up the bank quarterly financial statement that was lying on the coffee table.

I about fell out of my chair when I read it and learned that it was, indeed, Carl's bank. He owned the bank.

While I was recovering my composure, Carl showed up. When he introduced us to the bank president, Bo, it became old home week. Bo and I had sat next to each other on an American Airline's flight a few weeks earlier and had enjoyed a pleasant conversation.

While the four of us were visiting, I mentioned that I had always wanted to meet Amarillo Slim, a famous poker player and one of the early winners of the World Series of Poker (1972).

During the week we were in Amarillo, Carl and Bo sent us a constant stream of boot buyers, many of whom had never owned a pair.

On our second morning, there was a knock on the trailer door, and when I opened it, there stood Amarillo Slim. (Allow me to add that he did not look happy about being there.) Fortunately, Katie was a charmer, and Slim got hooked. He came back for coffee and to chat every morning until we left Amarillo.

The morning before we left town, he arrived considerably later than usual, and I asked him why he was late. Slim explained that he had been at the jail and had just left Cullen Davis's jail cell. Besides the weather, the hottest thing in Amarillo while we were there was the murder trial of T. Cullen Davis, a Fort Worth millionaire who was accused of murdering Stan Farr—the lover of Cullen's estranged wife Priscilla—at the Davis mansion in Fort Worth. Cullen's prominence in Fort Worth had caused the prosecution to be granted a change in venue for the murder trial, and Amarillo had been agreed upon as the location. That summer, Amarillo became the closest thing to a media circus Texas had seen in a long time.

The murder trial was of more than a passing interest to me. Stan's sister Linda (Texas Lil) had been a friendly competitor of my corporate dude ranch Ranchland, and Linda had been devastated by the loss of her brother. How or if Amarillo Slim and Cullen Davis were previously acquainted, I don't know, but I was curious about the reaction of Amarillo Slim—a great student of people, as are all great poker players. When I asked about his time at the jail with Cullen Davis, Amarillo Slim said, "I have a $20,000 bet that he will walk away from the trial a free man. I am totally comfortable with my bet, but I have never looked into the eyes of a guiltier son of a bitch in my life."

Davis was ultimately acquitted, a tribute to the fine lawyering of Houston's Richard "Racehorse" Haynes. The case was perhaps a precursor to the much more famous case involving O.J. Simpson. It's not hard to predict what the now-deceased Amarillo Slim would have said about that one, but I've never forgotten the importance of studying people.

There's always a market for excellence and quality.

My friend Claude, whom I originally met at the Harvard OPM program, shared with me that earlier in his business life—after achieving considerable success—he fell on hard times and nearly went broke. Determined to survive, Claude made the decision to fire sale his antique car collection, his art collection, and everything else he owned that wasn't essential.

What Claude discovered in the process provides a lesson that I consider very valuable. He told me that because he had to sell out virtually overnight to raise cash, he was not in a position to demand or receive top dollar on his assets. He said the very finest of the cars in his collection and the prized pieces in his art collection, the assets he had extravagantly paid top dollar for, were sold immediately and for significant profit. The so-so cars and the okay art were harder to sell and sold at a loss. One example he used was a pencil drawing he had by Picasso. Even though it was an original Picasso, the art community didn't consider it one of his finer works. Claude even lost money on that.

Every time I make a luxury investment purchase, I think of Claude's fire sale and walk away if I can't afford to buy the very best.

You can't create a market. Opportunity lies in identifying and serving unserved and underserved markets.

Without a doubt, one of the most valuable lessons I learned during the Harvard OPM program was from Professor Marty Marshall. He convinced all of us in the class that you cannot create a market—you can only serve one.

Ford's disastrous attempt to sell the Edsel is a great example of this wisdom. Typically, the most incredibly successful entrepreneurs identify a market that's not being served or is not being served well and move in to properly serve it. A good example is Levi Strauss, an immigrant who responded to the fact that California miners were so rough on their pants that they couldn't find pants strong enough to withstand the abuse of their work. Strauss originally used canvas, which was too harsh, and then settled on denim, which became an overnight success.

Another perhaps less obvious but outstanding opportunity lies in identifying a market that is being poorly served and serving it well. One such opportunity was found in public restrooms everywhere.

Introduced in 1948, World Dryer's hand dryer survived unchallenged for over fifty years. Their hand dryer sold for, depending on the model, around $300. Every entrepreneur who ever used one—that unfortunately includes me—should be absolutely ashamed of not immediately seeing the incredible opportunity that this high priced, inefficient, miserable piece of equipment offered. It was so bad that under the instructions where it told you to "Rub hands briskly in air stream," someone would frequently add, "Wipe hands on pants after use." Any thinking individual should have realized that a twenty-dollar hairdryer would do a better job at a fraction of the cost. Fortunately, Excel Dryer did recognize the opportunity, and they're rapidly replacing World Dryers in public restrooms everywhere.

— 10 —

Lessons from Harvard

I've mentioned several times the Harvard Business School's Owner/ President Management (OPM) program and the different lessons I learned. Enrolling into the program was one of the greatest learning experiences of my life. The Harvard Business School invites business owners from all over the world to attend the nine-week program; it is held three weeks each year for three consecutive years. In the early 1990s, the cost was $10,000 per year for each of the three years. I now understand that the yearly cost exceeds $30,000.

As an entrepreneur, it's inevitable that you will eventually be the only one who believes in a decision you've got to make. That means you've got to go against the grain and take risks.

In January 1991, I attended Harvard's OPM program. I had just sold Healthcare Staffing Resources to a New York Stock Exchange firm for several million dollars and was preparing to start my next company, Smart Start Inc. I shared the details of my plan with at least a dozen of my eighty-five classmates who hailed from thirty different countries.

It was fortunate that I had already learned the lesson of going against the grain and taking risks because not a single one of the dozen or so I shared my concept with felt it was a great business opportunity. I must admit that, at the end of our first month of business, we had one customer and sixty dollars in revenue. I had occasions to think back on many of their comments; however, I simply reminded myself that there is only one way to fail and that quite simply is to quit trying to win. I sold the company in 2006 to focus more time on helping seriously committed entrepreneurs grow their companies. I derive a great deal of pleasure from sharing with you that on August 21, 2015, the company sold again for $340 million— all cash. Today, Smart Start operates in eighteen countries, has 1.8 million customers, and is purported to be worth over $1 billion.

If you're going to jump in, do it with decisive action. My personal translation is, "Get big or get out."

While the Harvard professors were good, I believe that I learned more from the other entrepreneurs in attendance than the faculty. However, here are two specifics I did learn from Harvard professor Paul Vatter that proved to be worth far more than the cost of the entire three years. The first was the concept of BATNA. BATNA is an acronym standing for Best Alternative to a Negotiated Agreement.

I have always had a great deal of confidence in my negotiating skills, but those skills are of limited use when the other party is unwilling to negotiate when their BATNA is to do nothing. That was the dilemma facing my friend Norm.

Norm is an enormously wealthy, accomplished individual, the holder of forty-plus US patents, and the builder of a highly successful concrete and plastics businesses—now operated by his two sons Peter and Jon. One of Norm's many interests is aviation. He developed and received FAA approval for an $800,000 modification on the Piper Malibu airplane. Norm immediately recognized the value of what he had created but had little time to pursue it commercially. Instead, he identified three partners who had the facilities, tools, and expertise to modify the planes. The four of them formed a company to do the conversion. Norm's partners were, in fact, successful; but they were far from grateful. They were collectively in control of the recently formed company. They used their control to not pay dividends, to overpay themselves, and to sub work to a company they owned apart from Norm. Exasperated, Norm asked to be bought out. His partners offered only a small fraction of what Norm's interest was worth.

When Norm called me to complain about the treachery of his partners, I remembered the Harvard lesson on BATNA. I began to think about ways to compel the threesome to deal fairly with my friend. Rather than focusing on Norm's BATNA, I decided to change their BATNA which was to: (1) overpay themselves, (2) sub work to their other company, and (3) pay no dividends. Norm had formed Wallingford Associates LLC specifically to hold his equity in the venture, and he gave me complete control of Wallingford Associates.

I immediately wrote a nice letter to the terrible trio telling them that as the new CEO and President of Wallingford, I was looking forward to working with them. The response was exactly as I had anticipated. I received absolutely no response from any of my three FedExed letters. Thirty days later, having done my homework, I sent a second letter explaining that because of their paltry offer to buy Norm out and their unwillingness to communicate with me, I had been in touch with a major nonprofit that was exceptionally well-versed on minority positions, and that giving them all or part of Norm's ownership of Wallingford Associates would be much more financially rewarding to Norm than accepting their offer. In keeping with my conviction that the best bluff is no bluff at all, I attached the following letter.

Dear Mr. Rodgers,

Thank you for your recent phone call regarding your client's desire to possibly give The National Association for the Advancement of Colored People ("NAACP") a gift of stock.

Please feel free to contact our chief development officer to further discuss this potential gift.

Please do not hesitate to contact me should you require further assistance.

Very truly yours,

Deputy General Counsel

The sum result was that after drastically changing their BATNA, they bought Norm out for more than he and I had agreed he would accept.

The second valuable lesson I learned occurred during one of the fascinating professor-led exercises at the Harvard OPM program called "Two Pay Auction." In the exercise, we entrepreneur students engaged in an auction for a single fifty-dollar bill. Under the rules of the auction, a participant could only increase each bid by one dollar, and the party who won the auction received the fifty-dollar bill. The party who finished in second place was required to pay the amount of his final failed bid, and he received nothing. As the bidding neared the face amount of the fifty-dollar bill, it became clear that the final two bidders—everyone else had dropped out—would end up paying significantly more than fifty dollars for the fifty-dollar bill based on their desire to minimize their losses. As I recall, the winner paid seventy-five dollars for the fifty-dollar bill, and the loser ponied up seventy-four dollars for finishing second. The exercise was intended to demonstrate the dangers of gradualism.

Some years later, I recalled this lesson when I was on the Denton County Courthouse steps bidding on a commercial property that the sheriff was auctioning at a foreclosure sale. My only remaining opponent hesitantly and repeatedly raised my bid by one hundred dollars. After each raise, I immediately raised his bid by $2,000. My immediate and aggressive responses caused him to lose heart, and I bought the property for $97,000. Rental income from the property recovered my entire investment in three years. In the fourth year, I sold the property for over $500,000.

The best lesson from Harvard OPM

To the best of my knowledge, the Harvard Owners/Presidents Management program was, and remains, the only Harvard program directed specifically to entrepreneurs and small business owners. As I recall, there were eighty-six of us in my class and over two dozen countries were represented. Although I learned a good deal from the professors and even more from my fellow classmates, it became immediately clear that the professors and administrators in charge of the program were definitely neither entrepreneurs nor small business owners.

When I applied for the program, I had just signed a definitive agreement to sell Healthcare Staff Resources and needed to incur over $10,000 in additional company expenses before the closing or simply forfeit that money. Therefore, when I sent in my application, I sent a $10,000 check to cover the first year. Lo and behold, they sent the check back explaining that they could not accept payment until I had officially been accepted as a member of the program. I believe that then, and still today, the primary criteria for acceptance was being able to fog a mirror and sign a check. However, it took several phone calls and a great deal of persuasion to convince them that they could not teach an entrepreneurial program and not accept my check, which they finally did. At age eighty-two, I have yet to meet an intelligent small business owner or entrepreneur that, had they run the program, would not have cashed the check immediately.

One smart thing they did to make the classes more meaningful and valuable was to split the eighty-six of us into two groups and teach each class twice, thus allowing more interaction between students and the professors. When we arrived at the classroom on any given day, each desk had a card with our name on it. I soon realized they were setting the classrooms up for the following day immediately after that day's final class. Because there were several class members I wanted to get better acquainted with, some being close friends to this day, I frequently went down to the classrooms after dinner in the evening and did a bit of name card rearranging.

Professor Marty Marshall headed the teaching program at that time and was a very wise gentleman. As I mentioned earlier, one of the lessons he taught me that has proven valuable on numerous occasions throughout my career was that you cannot create a market, you can only serve one. A recent and humorous example of Marty's lesson is illustrated by a conversation I had with one of our city leaders, Andy Taft.

Mine and Bettye's primary home is a condo above the Omni Hotel, across from the convention center, in downtown Fort Worth. Fort Worth is an outstanding city. I'm a country boy at heart, and it's one of the very few cities I would ever consider living in. Early every morning when we are in town, I take our chocolate lab on a two-mile walk, most of which is on Main Street. Main Street provides an outstanding walk with trees and flowerbeds on the sidewalk next to the curb on nearly every block. As a result, most of the dog owners who live downtown walk their dogs on Main Street as I do. The flowerbeds have signs advising that dogs are not permitted to walk in them. At Rotary, Bettye became acquainted with and introduced me to Andy Taft, who was president of Downtown Fort Worth Inc. I pointed out to Andy that the city had created the perfect dog walk on Main Street; however, they had created it for a nonexistent market. It'd been created for dogs that neither had the need to pee or poop. I suggested the city replace a section of flowerbeds at every block with artificial turf. Andy tells me they like the idea and are in the process of executing it.

As Marty so wisely explained to us at Harvard: although you cannot create a market, there is a lot of money to be made in serving one.

— 11 —

Choose Your Battles and
Conduct Business with Respect

As mentioned previously, my friend Norm is the holder of forty-plus patents, and like other patent holders, he is occasionally involved in patent litigation. One particular patent fight with a competitor was galling, and Norm called me to get my input and guidance. As the case proceeded, we reached a point where Norm could pay his adversary $200,000 and walk away with everything he had hoped to achieve. I encouraged him to write the check, call it a win, and move on. Norm flatly refused to take my advice; pride was involved. Like many extremely wealthy individuals, Norm was prepared to spend extravagant amounts of money to ensure that he prevailed. Another six months into the fight, Norm did indeed prevail on all counts. When the fight was over, Norm cheerfully informed me that his adversary had to pay him $200,000. Norm proudly held out his chest as the victor.

Choose your fights carefully.
Are they really worth the time, effort, and expense?

From the time Norm could have paid $200,000 and gotten everything he wanted until he got what he wanted and received $200,000, his legal bill had gone up by well over $400,000.

The extremely wealthy can afford to spend that kind of money on ego and/or principles. Can you? I have actually written three negotiated-settlement checks when I felt I had an 80 percent chance of winning a lawsuit. Why?

1. **Lawsuits are time consuming**. They take you away from your core business.

2. **Lawsuits are negative.** Life is short, and a positive environment is worth a lot.

3. **The only sure winners are the lawyers.** The outcome is not always just, but the lawyers get paid regardless.

I have met with many entrepreneurs who think a patent is total protection for their unique product. It isn't! Unless you have extremely deep pockets, you may well go broke defending your patent. In my experience, patent litigation is the most expensive litigation of all.

If you maintain your ethics and integrity, you can disagree on business issues without destroying personal relationships.

The Godfather is considered by many to be the greatest American film ever made. Among the many quotable lines, one stands out: "It's not personal, Sonny. It's strictly business." The rationale for killing rivals is a classic line known to almost all moviegoers. If you're in the Mafia, this may work, but it's a foreign concept to those of us who don't make money by literally killing our competitors.

Business can be emotional, and by being emotional, it can become personal. The challenge lies in preventing business from becoming personal while, at the same time, remaining consistent with the business principles each of us establishes in conducting our business lives.

I have been involved in three national banks as an investor, board member, and chairman of the loan committee. That one bank was United Commerce Bank. I say three banks because United Commerce Bank was, is, and will remain: (1) my first bank involvement, (2) my last bank involvement, and (3) my only bank involvement.

I was one of the original investors and board members, and having opened the bank in the mid-1980s, we had many wild and exciting moments, battles with the regulators, and other crises. By 1991, the board was down from fourteen to a very functional seven members. As it happened, I had played a major role in attracting all but one of the seven board members to the bank. All of us were close friends.

I decided it was time to sell the bank. When I presented the idea, I was absolutely shocked to discover that all but one of my fellow directors and close friends were completely opposed to selling. The fight that followed ended up strengthening our bonds of friendship because we all retained our respect for one another. And, although vicious, it was a fight that no one lost.

Robert Fielder, the other director who was in favor of selling, and I both resigned from the board. I sought out and found a bank in a nearby larger city that wanted to buy our bank. I felt certain the shareholders at the upcoming annual meeting would be in favor of the sale and overshadow the board's desire. I was sure I had every-thing going my way, but the board had a trick up their sleeves too.

Although the sale got approved at the annual meeting, the board declared a cash dividend that reduced the assets of the bank by 15 percent. The almost laughable outcome was that the buyer honored his original offer despite the reduced value of the bank, and we all walked away friends with the additional money in our pocket as a result of our most honorable and enjoyable fight.

Less than two years after the sale, the directors who had opposed selling the bank opened a new bank within a mile of the one we sold. They even invited me to join as a founding director. I expressed my appreciation, but told them I had already had a lifetime's supply of banks and bank regulators.

This experience was a bit like my time in the army—I never want to do it again, but I sure enjoy looking back on it. To this day, when I'm about to get in a business fight, I remind myself that it's only business, it's not personal—and that maintaining my ethics and integrity are paramount.

If you deal with a skunk long enough, you are bound to get sprayed.

Have you ever done a deal with someone you didn't feel good about? Trust those instincts. Don't let greed or money cause you to do business with people you don't respect.

During the early years when I owned Ranchland, a farrier by the name of B. R. Blagg shod my horses. One day when he was not scheduled to shoe horses at my place, he showed up with a black horse. He knew I was a member of the Dallas Hella Temple Shriners Black Horse Patrol, and black horses that met the patrol's requirements were hard to find. Because I had a ranch near Dallas, many of the patrol members asked for my assistance when they needed a horse.

B. R. showed me his horse, and I immediately knew it had a better chance of being a dog's dinner than a Shriner's patrol horse. I didn't let on that I was shocked that he would present such a horse to me. Back in the 1960s, we were routinely paying from $2,500 to $5,000 for our mounts in the patrol. I was sure that at the local auction his horse would sell by the pound and bring $300 to $400. B. R. told me he was asking $3,500 for the horse. I said, "B. R., I want you to load up your horse, get off my property, and never come back."

Totally shocked, and perhaps thinking about the immediate loss of a portion of his farrier's revenue, he asked why. I told him that I couldn't afford to have anyone around me who thought so little of me as to try to sell me a $400 horse for $3,500.

This experience prompted me to receive a gift I've enjoyed throughout my business life. It was a gift I gave myself: I vowed that, in the future, I would not do business with anyone that I didn't respect and somewhat enjoyed being around. The gift has definitely made my business life much more enjoyable, and I personally believe it has made my business dealings more financially rewarding.

Life is short. Life is more fun if you surround yourself with business associates you respect, trust, and enjoy working with. All the great deals I have ever done have happened with extremely smart people on the other side of the table. As I said at the beginning of this book—and it bears repeating—winning a deal fifty-one to forty-nine is not near as much fun as losing fifty-nine to sixty-one because smart, win-win entrepreneurs figure out how to add twenty points to the total value.

— 12 —

Cover Your Bases

In a service business, defining your market upfront is one of the keys to profitability. Because the time and expense of employee travel to customer locations can be a significant cost to your business, it's important to distinguish between the desirability of certain business and the circumstances under which you will accept less desirable (less profitable) business.

Define your market on the front end, and don't lose money trying to be all things to all people.

In an in-home, nonmedical assisted living business I started with my sister-in-law, Becci, we drew two concentric circles around the company's headquarters, which we located within our primary market in select Dallas zip codes where wealthy, older residents lived.

Within the first circle, we marketed by direct mail and accepted any staffing assignment—even one- and two-hour, unprofitable jobs with new customers. Additionally, we spent major time and money interviewing clients and ensuring that we matched the client with the most appropriate caregiver for their personality and needs.

Within the second circle, we did not expend money to market but would accept minimum four-hour-long assignments that came to us by referral or word-of-mouth. Outside the two circles, we would accept business only at negotiated rates, which were immediately profitable for our company. In this manner, we directed our marketing efforts to the area we most desired to serve, therefore limiting the costs of expanding beyond that core market only to those situations most profitable to us. Within the first circle, we became the provider of choice and frequently had clients ask us to raise our fees so that their caregiver would get a raise.

Get it right. Choose a tagline and logo that is simple, memorable, and descriptive.

Naming your company and adopting an effective tagline deserves a great deal more attention than it frequently receives. When naming a small or startup business, don't be led astray by the names of major corporations. Coca-Cola is a good name only because at this point virtually all the world's population recognizes it.

Unfortunately, there's a big temptation to substitute initials for the name of a business. IBM gets away with this because most of the business world recognizes International Business Machines Inc. The Entrepreneurs' Organization, a worldwide organization for entrepreneurs with chapters in forty countries, has fallen into the bad habit of calling themselves EO. Using the initials rather than the name of the organization is, in my opinion, a huge mistake. It's very convenient for all those who are familiar with Entrepreneurs' Organization, but it offers absolutely no meaning to the people they want to attract as new members. You must maintain a constant vigil to prevent initials from replacing your company name. One startup that I originally

116

had total-voting control of we named Physician Staffing Resources. We started the company with the CEO and one paid assistant. At its pinnacle, that company had 275 employees and managed over 2,000 ER physicians. Despite my best efforts, the company's functional name is PSR.

When George Eastman founded Kodak, he intended it to be a worldwide company and, therefore, picked a name that was easy to pronounce in most languages, was pronounced the same in all languages, and had no negative connotations in any language.

Hopefully you'll devote as much thought to naming your company as George did.

My sister-in-law and I named the Nashville-based, in-home, nonmedical assisted living business Elderly Services Inc. I like company names that help people understand what the company does or sells. Originally, I thought Elderly Services Inc. was a brilliant name; unfortunately (much to my chagrin) when we opened up for business, we quickly learned that nobody becomes "elderly" until about twenty minutes before they die. Our tagline "Stay in charge and at home—never spend a single night in a nursing home" was some help in mitigating the disaster of our chosen name. We did manage to prosper, but it was no thanks to the name.

We sold the company, which we had started with just a few thousand dollars, for over $1 million three years later. When we sold, we agreed to a noncompete in the Nashville market. Therefore, we opened our next in-home staffing facility in the Dallas, Texas, market. Having learned the painful naming lesson well, we named the new venture Family Staffing Solutions. I'm happy to report that Family Staffing Solutions became many, many times more successful than Elderly Services Inc.

A company that I've mentioned before, which my wife Bettye and I started together, was another company whose name worked very well: Smart Start. The Smart Start ignition interlock device in cars was normally ordered by the court as a requirement for convicted DUI and DWI offenders to legally drive. As previously mentioned, the device required them to blow into a unit measuring their breath alcohol before the car would start. The logo for Smart Start was a stylized traffic light with the green, yellow, and red circles.

When we started the company, Mothers Against Drunk Driving (MADD) still believed that all drunk drivers should be thrown in jail and the cell key thrown away. (As a side note, MADD created a very effective name by using initials.) Smart Start played a significant role in convincing MADD and the judicial system that it was neither cost-effective nor socially desirable to use lengthy incarceration as a solution to drunk driving. Attempting to reform the large population of longtime heavy drinkers was also not a practical approach.

We promoted the fact that the goal was to save lives being lost in traffic accidents caused by alcohol. It wasn't necessary to change their drinking habits to accomplish the goal. All we needed to do was to make sure they did not drive when drinking. This thinking brought about the tagline for Smart Start: "Separating Drinking from Driving." Having played a major role in over twenty startups, the Smart Start tagline is, in my opinion, by far the best I have ever written.

Focus on sales and marketing value when you're naming your company or writing taglines. Think of your prospective customers and how they will be impacted by the name and/or tag line.

Do your due diligence, do your research, and be aware of what's out there.

My friend and fellow bank director Jim owned a company that sold uninterrupted power supplies and surge protectors. His company was growing, and he needed a larger building. Jim called me one day to ask that I evaluate a building he was seriously considering purchasing.

Unfortunately, three other real estate agents were already involved in the deal, so as a real estate agent, I concluded that there was no more room for a commission for me in this transaction. But I still agreed to evaluate his prospective new location. As I always do when looking at real estate, I also looked at the surrounding properties as well as the one I had been requested to tour. The building next door was so similar to the desired property that I went in to look around. After proceeding through most of this occupied location, I was intercepted by the office manager. His mission was to quickly and politely throw me out. As he was leading me to the front door, we passed what was obviously the boss's office. I detoured into that office. The manager, not realizing that I was no longer following him, continued on without me. I quickly introduced myself to the boss, and by the time the manager realized I wasn't following him and returned to retrieve me, the boss waved him off and we continued our friendly conversation.

The boss told me that he owned both the business and the building. I explained that my friend was looking for a building like his and was considering the building next door, and that I would appreciate any insight he might offer about the building and the area. The boss explained that he had actually been considering selling his building, but he had not put it on the market because he hadn't quite determined how to deal with a foundation problem. By the time I left,

I knew what the foundation problem was and what the boss wanted for his building. I then went by Jim's office and suggested that he look at this building before closing on the next-door property. Jim looked at the building, felt it was ideal for his company and—having an engineering background—believed the foundation problem was not nearly as serious as the price discount it generated. Jim bought the building, and I received all the commission on the full $500,000 purchase price.

A similar situation occurred with respect to a property I owned and wanted to sell. This was one of two properties I had received in lieu of foreclosure. Because I had worked with this debtor in good faith—as I had with all of them—when he was unable to pay his note, he gave me the deed on a vacant lakeside lot at Lake Kiowa, Texas—a small, gated community a few miles south of the Oklahoma-Texas border. By telephone, I engaged a real estate agent whose office was located just outside the gates of Lake Kiowa to list my property and hopefully identify its ultimate buyer. After six-to-eight weeks of no activity, on a Saturday morning, I decided to drive up and look at this property I now owned. After convincing the guard at the front gate that I was a property owner, he gave me access and pointed me in the general direction of my lot.

When I arrived, there was nothing much to see. It looked like all the other lakefront lots. I did notice the next-door neighbor was mowing his lawn. When I approached him, he cut off the mower to talk. I told him that I now owned the lot next door, didn't know anything about local real estate values, and asked him what he thought my lake lot property was worth. He was reluctant to give me a price, and I finally asked, "How much would you pay believing you were buying it way below market?"

With that, he gave me a price, and I simply said, "Sold."

He offered to get his checkbook to write an earnest money check. I suggested that he wait until Monday morning and drop by the real estate agent's office to work up a contract. So, I sold my property to my next-door neighbor in all of fifteen minutes, and my real estate agent received a not-so-deserved full commission on the sale.

These two sales illustrate a fundamental principle of mine regarding real estate transactions: never casually dismiss the owners of adjacent properties. In many cases, they are the world's leading experts on the property you're looking at. This principle frequently applies to non-real-estate ventures as well. Often people standing quietly on the sidelines can provide valuable information.

Taking time to contact the debtor and asking if he or she would like me to buy their loan totally changes the relationship and dynamics.

In the late 1980s, bank regulators decided that many banks had bad loans and weren't financially solid. The regulators made Texas their first target. Banks that were deemed unsound were closed or sold. Many loans were shipped to major financial institutions in far-off cities. As a result, people who could were often able to buy their loans back for a fraction of the amount owed. Those who couldn't afford to buy their loans were at the mercy of the bank.

The regulators sold weak banks to other sound banks. Banks that bought these banks were given allowances on specific classified loans. To get rid of the bad loans, the banks could sell them at huge discounts and still break even while getting bad loans off of their books and cleaning up their loan portfolios.

I became involved when two brothers came to me for help after their local bank sold and the new owner called in all four of their loans. Their bank had been purchased by the Ford Group that owned several banks. In the course of helping the brothers, I became acquainted with Alan Cawthon, the new president of their bank. Alan told me the bank owned several classified loans.

I looked at the loans that were available for sale and asked Alan if I committed to buy several of the loans, would he be willing to modify the loan terms before I took them? Alan said that wouldn't be a problem as long as the debtors agreed.

I picked out the loans that I wanted and went to each debtor to tell them that I was looking at buying a group of loans from their bank and that their loans were among them. I explained that, per the fine print in their loan documents, their note was a negotiable instrument that the bank could sell without their consent. However, I had a personal rule that I would never buy a person's loan unless they wanted me to. I was there to determine if they wanted me to buy their note.

Everyone I visited with was mad at the bank for calling their loans, so it was an easy question. I took it a step further and asked what they didn't like about the terms of the loan and why they would like me to buy it: some needed longer amortization periods to reduce their monthly payment, some knew the notes were selling at a discount and wanted the option to pay off the note early at a reduced price, and some were so upset at the bank that they were happy for me to buy their note(s) with no changes.

In many cases, I revised the amortization schedules to lower monthly payments. In some cases, I agreed to sell them the note later at a discount, or made other adjustments to enlist their support and enthusiasm. I had the bank make all the adjustments so that I didn't have to mess with the paperwork.

Out of the approximately eighty notes I bought at between 20 percent and 70 percent of their face value, I never lost a single cent on any note—including two instances where we later agreed on a deed in lieu of foreclosure.

Leverage your loyalty.

I was understandably excited about owning my first Lexus. A high-end, luxury vehicle is a source of joy to any car aficionado. Its bells and whistles offer countless opportunities for amazement, amusement, and even frustration at their complexities.

I bought my first Lexus—a 1990 model—from a Fort Worth dealer in 1989, the year Lexus was introduced in the US. The magnitude of the expense did, however, make me wonder if I might have purchased at a better price in another market.

On a flight to London the following year, I found myself seated next to Carl Sewell, the owner of one of the most successful Lexus dealerships in North Texas and author of *Customers for Life*. Our conversation naturally turned to my Lexus and the fact that I was intending to trade it for another new Lexus sedan next year. Carl made it clear that the Sewell Lexus policy was to rely on its well-deserved reputation for customer service as the basis for holding the line on the purchase price of each and every vehicle. I got the clear impression that the demand for Lexus vehicles in the DFW market was so strong that none of the dealers were offering much of a price concession.

When the time came to purchase my second Lexus, I dutifully collected quotes from Sewell Lexus and two other North Texas Lexus dealerships. All the quotes were within $500 of each other. In the midst of shopping for my new car, I flew to San Antonio on an overnight business trip. After the meeting, I was in my hotel room early with time on my hands. In those days, the hotel rooms still had *Yellow Pages*, and I ended up looking up the local Lexus dealership. The dealership had just changed hands, and I was fortunate enough to get the new general manager on the phone. When I asked him if he was serious about selling cars, he explained that his company had just acquired the dealership, the lot was overflowing, and he was extremely serious. I told him in that case, while on my way to the airport the next day, I would have the cab make a small detour and stop at his dealership. This was in 1991. When I stopped, I told the cab to wait.

Less than five minutes after I shook hands with the new manager, I had purchased my new Lexus. He set the allowance for my trade-in based on its mileage and my description of its condition. I told him that he could deduct from the trade-in allowance any amount he thought was appropriate after he saw the car. He accepted my proposal, and the following week, my new car was delivered to me at my office north of Dallas. He didn't request any deductions after seeing my car, and I purchased that car for $5,000 less than my best DFW offer.

Since that time, I have purchased over fifty new Lexus from the dealer for myself, my wife, my attorney, my CPA, and a couple of other close friends—all of which the dealership has delivered to Dallas. Service is important, but sometimes it pays to shop around.

Being a loyal customer also has its perks, as I found out when I needed a new pickup. Because I had been so happy with all of my

Lexus vehicles (made by Toyota), I decided to buy a new Toyota pickup. Shortly after taking delivery, Bettye pointed out that my new truck was leaking oil on our driveway. I returned the truck to the dealer. As it turned out, the camshaft had not been properly installed and major repairs were required. The dealer informed me that they would have it repaired within a few days.

My response was, "Fix it? Like hell you will. I paid for a new truck, and I want a new truck."

The dealer responded that they just couldn't do that. I told them to hold the truck, do nothing to it without my authorization, and that I would send them further instructions from my office that afternoon.

When I returned to my office, I pulled out the records on the, at that time, forty-plus Lexus I had been involved in purchasing. I faxed the list, complete with VIN numbers of each vehicle, to the dealership. I'm sure you won't find it hard to believe that the next morning they called to inform me that they would be delivering a brand new truck to my office that day.

The time to address your concerns is before you sign on the dotted line. Do your due diligence and look for ways to reduce your risk.

When Bettye and I were looking to buy the downtown Fort Worth condo being built above the newly opened, fifteen-story Omni Hotel, Bob Rowling—the owner of the Omni sixty-property hotel chain—had just started marketing the eighty-seven condo units, as they were still several months away from completion. At that point, the residential real estate market was extremely hot. I was dragging my feet regarding committing to a unit and putting up a deposit. When the sales agent pressed, wanting to know why that with our apparent strong interest we had not moved ahead, I explained I was concerned that the market was overheated, the bubble might well burst, and they would need to lower prices. Because this project was by far the highest-per-square-foot residential property in Fort Worth, I thought it was especially vulnerable. I was immediately assured that Bob was funding the project out of pocket and would never lower the prices.

My response was, "That's wonderful. I will get back to you tomorrow afternoon."

The next morning, I met with David Hammer, my M&A attorney, and he drafted a beautiful clause for me that provided a rebate equal to any reduction in the current published unit prices: If a unit sold at a price 9 percent below the currently listed price, I would receive a check for 9 percent of my purchase price. If later a unit sold at a 14 percent reduction, I would receive another 5 percent, and on and on.

The next afternoon, I met with the condo sales manager, and much to my surprise, they agreed to include my clause in the contract. As I have said many times, ask and you may-shall-will receive.

When the market did fall, Mike, Bob's right-hand man, contacted me and told me that Bob would like to buy out my clause. I offered to sell it for $172,500. I knew that although most units were being reduced only about 7 to 9 percent, the least expensive unit in the project was being reduced from $399,000 to $299,000 as a loss leader and means of advertising "from $299,000."

Later that week, Mike called. He explained that the previous night he and Bob had flown in from Houston on the company plane and had discussed my $172,500 offer. Mike told me that Bob wanted to counter and was prepared to pay $100,000. I simply said, "That's not acceptable. However, I'll be contacting the sales office tomorrow as I've decided to buy the $299,000 unit."

The next morning, I got wind of a rumor at the Omni of which the gist was: "Good news! We have a buyer for the unit on the sixteenth floor. Bad news: Jay Rodgers is the buyer, and his net cost will be $35,000."

Later that morning, I got a call from Mike, asking if I was really serious about buying the second unit. My reply was, "Yes. Under the circumstances, I feel it is the thing to do." After a pause, I continued. "However, I am willing to"—at that point, I could almost visualize Mike leaning closer to the phone—"reopen my original offer for twenty-four hours."

I received a check for $172,500, and as a rebate (reduction in purchase price), it wasn't even subject to taxes.

When you're recruiting for your company, seize the moment. As my Welsh friend taught me, "Cut a walking stick when you find it."

Many of my companies had experienced ongoing difficulties in identifying and hiring qualified sales personnel. Because I believe that you can't pay a good salesman too much, I knew our difficulties were not with our pay structure; rather, we didn't do a good job in qualifying our prospective employees.

I was in Las Vegas one day attending a seminar on sales. One of the speakers was a Dallas man named Tom. Tom talked about the importance of preemployment testing to determine if an individual was likely to succeed in sales. His presentation impressed me, and I believed that he could help us solve our longstanding problem with the lackluster performance of, and the resulting turnover among, our sales staff.

When Tom completed his presentation, I approached the platform and asked him if I might take a few minutes of his time. Tom replied that he was headed to the airport right away to return home to Dallas. I asked if I might join him on his cab ride to the airport so we could talk further. He agreed, and we talked all the way to the airport. When we arrived, I felt there was still more to learn, so I changed my return ticket and joined him. When we boarded the plane, I persuaded the person sitting next to Tom to change seats with me. By the time we landed, Tom was on the team.

Ever since then, Tom has screened and interviewed all of our sales candidates, and the results have been spectacular. Additionally, Tom donates his time and talent as a powerful guest speaker at our Biz Owners Ed program.

Understand the tax laws and understand your rights. You can live a good deal longer and/or better on the same income if Uncle Sam isn't sharing a big paycheck with you.

Many young entrepreneurs put their money in their start-up business alongside investor money. They then immediately begin drawing a salary sufficient to support themselves. Your tax advisor may tell you that you need to take some salary. If so, take the absolute minimum amount required. Rather than putting your cash in the business, with either an LLC or Sub S, you can buy your percent of the equity for a fraction of what the other investors pay. This allows you to put the rest of your funds aside and live on them free of payroll taxes. Likewise, you can loan the balance of the money to the company and live on the monthly repayment paying taxes only on the interest.

— 13 —

Established Entrepreneurs Still Learn

For many years, I was an active member of the Dallas chapter of the CEO Club. The CEO Club, like many executive organizations, seeks to create peer-to-peer networks of executives so that each member may benefit from the experience and advice of their fellow members. At CEO Club meetings, one member presents his company in-depth, and the other members then present their thoughts, comments, and suggestions.

Don't let "big" overshadow "profitable."

In those presentations, I noticed a disturbing tendency to focus on gross revenue rather than on bottom-line profit. After one presentation by my friend Aggie, I said, "Aggie, you have laid out a great plan for huge revenue growth over the next three years; however, I did not hear a single reference to net income. The stock market—through its quoted P/E ratio and, in most cases, buyers of small businesses through their use of EBITDA multiples—values companies based upon their bottom lines, not their top lines. As comforting as it is to view growth in revenue numbers, you're misleading yourself if that's the way you're choosing to plan your growth and measure success. Most revenue belongs to other people or companies, and you are required to handle, process, and account for it. Only that small portion of revenue that makes it to the bottom line is yours to spend. Personally, I think your growth plan should be built around growing net profits, and the need to handle more revenue is just one of the unfortunate requirements."

Every new technology or advancement isn't necessarily a good deal. Evaluate software not based on the bells and whistles. Evaluate it based on your bottom line.

Technology can be a wonderful tool in two situations: first, the software must be capable of accomplishing the purpose for which you acquired it; second, you (or your appropriate employee[s]) must be able to use it efficiently. For these reasons, I avoid what the tech people refer to as bleeding-edge technology and leading-edge technology. While some technophiles simply must have the latest, greatest anything, the extreme high cost, the productivity lost, the associated problems, and the longer learning curve frequently make it unprofitable. Business is, after all, about profit. (If you doubt that, try giving your church a share of your losses.) I believe in using technology that is proven to increase productivity. Only then should company resources be dedicated to training your employee base in its application to your business.

If at all possible, avoid falling into the trap of software development. If your business is large enough, somewhere in it there will be an IT person who knows they can build exactly what your company needs. Worse yet, your IT person may have an IT friend, or may have read about an IT developer, who can certainly build what you need.

If you fall into this trap, forget about the metrics of "on time" and "under budget." You almost certainly will not experience either. And when you don't, the shininess of your new toy will dim significantly as time goes by, and the cost overruns increase. When you buy software, buy results that are valuable to your company.

I always say, "I'll pay you when I push a button and X happens . . . not when you tell me the marvelous things you have achieved." When you use software off the shelf, a company supports it. When you contract to develop software specifically for your company, or even if you develop it internally, the developer being away on a fishing trip may shut down production, and one heart attack may destroy its ongoing value. That heart attack can potentially even leave the company in dire straits.

Few businesses truly require custom software development. Yours, in all likelihood, is not one of them.

Be careful if you have a one-trick pony. Success often eludes the one-trick pony. Look for more tricks or another buyer.

My longtime friend John invested in a computer software company that provided a management and accounting program for college and university dormitories. It covered both student and outside summer-resident groups. The company's underlying technology was sound, but the company was bedeviled by the lengthy sales cycle associated with public and private colleges and universities. It was not unusual for this company to call on its prospective customers for five years or even longer before concluding a sale. The CEO jokingly talked about prospective academic institutions that belonged to their five-year club. Because they sold only the one software product, the cost of producing a sale was devastating to their profitability.

John convinced me to get involved when he offered me 20 percent of the company stock to join the board and focus on their success. It did not take long to determine that the sales expense had to be drastically reduced if they were to become profitable. The two options I focused on for accomplishing that were either: (1) adding several, much-less expensive items to their product line that could be sold to the same academic prospects on a first or second call basis, or (2) selling the company to a well-established organization that was already calling on our prospects and sold a wide range of products. We settled on the latter option. A buyer was identified, a sale was concluded, and the company's technology finally had a real chance to succeed in the market.

Learning a few new tricks.

At age eighty on January 2, 2020, I sold my most recent startup: a company called Track What Matters—DBA Rhino Fleet Tracking. I was delighted to find out that even old dogs such as myself can learn new tricks. Having sold all my previous companies based on a multiple of EBITDA, I felt the company should bring somewhere in the neighborhood of five times EBITDA. I was excited to learn that, unlike any of my previous companies, Rhino was a software as a service (SAAS) company, and they sold at a multiple of annual reoccurring revenue rather than a multiple of EBITDA. I believe the fact that it was a SAAS company and two decisions I made account for the company selling for fifty times the trailing twelve months EBITDA and I—as I write this book at age eighty-two—finally fully understand the meaning of SAAS.

The first of those two decisions was deciding to hire Founders Advisors out of Birmingham, Alabama, as our investment banking firm. We had approached four different firms for a proposal, and all four had flown in a team that spent half a day presenting the reasons they should be awarded the assignment to our board. A firm out of Denver was the board's leading choice (not mine) until we received their letter of agreement. Despite the agreement calling for us to pay them a five-figure monthly fee, their agreement provided that they would be paid in full even if they were fired before a sale took place and the buyer was a company they had not introduced. Additionally, their agreement was about twelve pages, nine or ten of which were devoted to CYA. The Founders Advisors' proposal was four or five pages, and the majority of it focused on how we would work together to sell the company.

The second decision I made was based on my long-held belief that buyers are always concerned that when the sellers walk away with their money, they will also be walking away with expertise and management skills that will reduce the value of the company. I frequently tell mentees that, especially in the last year or two before they sell their company, the more vacations they take and the longer they are, the more their company will be worth.

Once we had hired the investment banking firm, I told our board that, going forward, neither I nor any board member would ever communicate in any way with any prospective buyer. Mike Brown and Steven Van Ooyen ran the company and were not only staying on after the sale but were also investing a portion of the profit from their stock in the buyer's company. They would handle all communications with prospective buyers. This made it clear to the buyers that none of the investors were involved in the company's success. The investors were simply a group of old folks trying to get liquid and put their estates in order before they passed.

Timing is critical when soliciting donations for worthy causes.

All successful entrepreneurs end up being involved in nonprofits and charity work. Raising money for these entities is a never-ending task. This story is to provide you with some of the lessons I've learned and an approach that you may well find powerfully effective. It is all about timing.

When Smart Start sold in 2015 for $340 million, all cash, I had previously sold my stock, but I reached out to the shareholders I had brought aboard in the beginning. This is where timing comes in. The day they received the bank wire paying them for their stock, they also received a letter from me, reminding them that a great way to celebrate their incredible windfall was by donating to Biz Owners Ed. That letter generated well over $100,000 in donations. One shareholder, Dr. Nishendu Vasavada, who received a check for approximately $4 million on his $25,000 investment, donated $50,000 to Biz Owners Ed.

The letter I wrote worked so well that I wrote a similar one to Track What Matters shareholders when we sold that company early in 2020 for $25 million cash.

Dear Fellow Shareholders,

The sale of Track What Matters has finally been concluded, and your funds have been wired. What a magnificent way to start the new year! As you are all well aware over the years in all of the investments that I have envisioned and overseen, I never asked for or accepted any compensation for the mountain of hours I have spent finding, structuring, and nurturing these investments. Your return on each dollar invested is identical to my return. I mention this because I'd like you to join Bettye and me in celebrating our great entrepreneurial win by making a significant donation to Biz Owners Ed, our nonprofit dedicated to helping serious, committed entrepreneurs grow their companies, create jobs, and support all that has made our country great and our personal lives unbelievably incredible.

January 7, 2020, will be the opening evening of the eighth year of Biz Owners Ed's ten-week program. I would like to open the program by announcing each of your personal contributions to Biz Owners Ed. If necessary to ensure that your donation arrives in time, please FedEx your check made payable to Biz Owners Ed to me.

Thank you for your support,

Jay D. Rodgers

This letter also generated major contributions to Biz Owners Ed. I'm happy to report that shareholder Dr. Vasavada contributed an additional $25,000 on this occasion. Again, timing is critical when you are conducting a fundraising campaign. For instance, don't waste your energy soliciting in early April at tax time. On the day everyone received the letter from me, they had won big with the sale of our company and were most likely to feel grateful and ready to share their good fortune.

— 14 —

Thank Yous

Having mentored individuals for over four decades, taught the Starting Your Own Business course at the University of North Texas, written numerous entrepreneurial articles, and presented at Southern Methodist University's entrepreneurial master's program, I have received hundreds of thank you notes, letters, and emails over the years.

I always tell mentees that, although I might be able to give them the absolute best solution to their problem, if my suggestion doesn't fit them, feel right, or if they're not comfortable pursuing it, it's probably not the best approach for them to take.

The exception and the one thank you note that I cherish above all others I received from Annye Grande. Early on, I believed she was going to take her company to the moon and, therefore, spent a great deal more time over several years mentoring her. Annye had been in the fashion world for many years when she launched her luxury handbag line under the brand name Etoile.

I am a good friend of David Marold, who runs the Bohlin company. Edwin Bohlin initially became famous in the 1930s and 1940s, when he made leather goods for virtually all the top Western movie stars in Hollywood. His goldsmiths and silversmiths adorned their parade saddles with conchos, corner plates, and other incredible pieces of art that are still sought after today. The company and the talent relocated many years ago to Dallas. Today, Bohlin's primary focus is on exquisite Western belt buckles. However, in 2017, David paid tribute to their tradition of fine Western saddles by building a saddle for one of his customers that was laden with gold and silver and sold for $250,000.

Because I knew David was a master at marketing to the absolute top of the high-end clientele, I tried unsuccessfully on several occasions to connect Annye and David. They exchanged an email or two, and I think spoke once on the phone, but never had a face-to-face sit down. One afternoon when Annye was in my office, I picked up the phone, put it on speaker, called David, and said, "I'm damn tired of you two not getting together. I just told Annye she's not welcome back in my office until you two meet."

When they did, it was immediately a business match made in heaven. Annye currently has a handbag being produced that will feature some of Bohlin's finest work. I always tell mentees that if it doesn't feel good and fit them, don't do it. All rules are meant to occasionally be broken; this was one of those times.

Annye's thank you note:

July 16, 2021

Dear Jay,

I want to thank you for insisting that I visit with David Marold at Bohlin. David was generous of his time, and his detailed explanation of their exquisite handmade products was enlightening. We have multiple retail accounts that cross as well as some of the same luxury trunk show events.

Furthermore, David will be able to produce a specialty hardware I have been trying to source for over a year. I am thrilled!

In conclusion, when Jay Rodgers tells you to stop being an ass and connect with someone, there is a good reason. So just do it!

Thank you for putting up with me,

Annye

After Annye had worked with David to create her new handbag, she sent me this follow-up email:

Dear Jay,

I am writing you this follow-up note to thank you again for your insistence that I get out of my own way and connect with David Marold once and for all.

In the last year we have visited multiple times, and David has turned into one of my FAVORITE PEOPLE of all time.

Business wise, his knowledge and experience has been INSTRUMENTAL in the success of the niche category Etoile added to the collection last year.

Furthermore, we are also collaborating on designing an exclusive collection for his brand.

I am extremely grateful for the introduction, but I am more grateful for the fact that you took the time to personally intervene and made sure this meeting would happen.

You sincerely care about our ultimate success without agenda or expecting anything in return and that is what gives entrepreneurs like me wings.

I am attaching two pictures of the collection David helped with.

Thank you so much,

Annye

Biz Owners Ed

While I have moved out of the leadership role of Biz Owners Ed, it is still incredibly important to me, and I want as many people as possible to be aware of it and, perhaps, duplicate its success.

Biz Owners Ed was created because a small group of highly successful entrepreneurs believed in small business and the benefits it provides to America's economy and society. This group knew there were numerous entrepreneurs out there who shared their belief and who were willing and eager to give back to, help perpetuate, and help expand this country's seriously committed entrepreneurs by sharing advice from lessons they had learned.

The idea was originally conceived by me because I appreciate the impact entrepreneurs can have on this country. I have spent a great deal of time over the years mentoring entrepreneurs one-on-one. I wanted to have a more powerful impact and a greater influence on more people than I could have with my own limited time. So I stepped back and asked, "What can I devote the rest of my life to that would give ongoing, perpetual motion to the fostering and support of successful entrepreneurship?" By leveraging my own circle of friends and business associates, Biz Owners Ed was born.

I initially enlisted the support of my wife, Bettye, David Hammer, Jim Attrell, Rick Garrett, and Dave Casey as cofounders. They all shared a concern about the tremendous growth in governmental control of businesses, which is moving America away from the free enterprise system that has made our country the greatest country in the world. Although I have invested the majority of my time the last twenty-plus years to helping entrepreneurs, I found I was spending too much time with people who weren't committed or serious enough about building the jobs and creating companies in the private sector that are the backbone of our country's greatness.

The founders recognized an enormous need for support for serious learners, devoted entrepreneurs, and disciplined high achievers by providing opportunities for them to learn from expert advisors who have successfully dealt with the same challenges they are facing.

Higher education was not the answer. Although the higher education system and its tenured professors are well qualified to teach science, literature, history, and many other subjects, most of the professors have never agonized over how they were going to make the next payroll or fund a company's progress. Most have probably never mortgaged their home and future to keep their company alive. Therefore, they're neither equipped nor able to provide the support required for teaching entrepreneurship. Although I taught the Starting Your Own Business course at the University of North Texas and was a guest speaker at the Caruth Institute for Entrepreneurship at Southern Methodist University's Cox School of Business, I felt I could make a bigger impact in a different setting with a different audience.

Designing and developing the program took over a year and a half, and the first class assembled on January 8, 2013. The class is limited to only twelve members each year so that the participants can interact with the presenters. However, applicants who aren't selected for a seat in the class are invited to audit the program from the gallery.

They are not allowed to interact with the presenters during his or her presentation; otherwise, they enjoy all the program's wisdom and benefits. The guiding principles for selecting class members are: (1) their business brings in over $1 million a year in revenue [$20 million is on the high end], (2) they have been in business fewer than seven years, and (3) they have a major ownership in their company. There is one more guideline, and it is the only one cast in concrete: the selection committee must be totally convinced of the individual's commitment and dedication to growing his or her company and creating a multiple of the company's current number of employees. Currently, there is no charge for the selected class members to attend all ten, four-hour-long, Tuesday evening class sessions. However, they must pay a (conditionally) refundable deposit of $1,500 when accepted. The conditions for a full refund are: (1) they must not miss any sessions [$500 is deducted from their deposit refund for each session they miss], and (2) they must not be late to any session [$100 is deducted for each time they are even one minute late].

Biz Owners Ed has a full slate of exceptional mentors who are willing and eager to give back and help new entrepreneurs. The organization's criteria for inviting mentors to participate in the program are that: (1) they have built from humble beginnings at least one megamillion-dollar company [some have built two, three, and more], (2) they commit to give their time and knowledge, and (3) they will make one or two presentations during the ten-week program. Out-of-state mentors are only required to present as their travel schedule permits. Additionally, as an indication of their sincere desire to help entrepreneurs, they must write a $5,000 check to the Business Owners Ed 501(c)(3) nonprofit organization when accepted as a mentor. It is significant that more than 80 percent of the individuals invited by Biz to become mentors have accepted the invitation. Many go beyond the ten-week formal program and have established ongoing mentor/mentee relationships with its graduates.

The Biz Owners Ed team is very deliberate and cautious about inviting guest speakers, most of whom own businesses that service and support small businesses. Guest speakers are there to provide only immediate and actionable information of value to entrepreneurs, not to solicit in any form or fashion clients for their particular businesses. Any guest speaker uttering a single solicitous line during the presentation is not invited back.

The Biz Owners Ed program is a great platform for entrepreneurs to get honest feedback from their peers and from entrepreneurs who have already achieved success. This program should be in every major city because it helps entrepreneurs grow their businesses and create more private-sector, small-business jobs. In every session, entrepreneurs are inspired so much by the stories shared and the advice they get that it changes their business.

If you have already climbed your entrepreneurial mountains, maybe you should start a Biz Owners Ed type program of your own to help mentor other entrepreneurs. You can contact Biz by visiting the website: www.BizOwnersEd.org. The founders are willing and anxious to help you launch your program. Because the program's only goal is to help seriously committed entrepreneurs, your program does not even need to mention Biz Owners Ed's support.

— 16 —

Lessons at a Glance

- Entrepreneurs do what it takes to accomplish the goal.
- Be different! Stand out! It may take a few trial-and-error moments at first. When you play to win big, you won't win them all, but you won't get lost in the crowd. Keep the momentum going. Always learn, be proactive, and be willing to make a move.
- Entrepreneurs always find a way. Sometimes it's not the normal way or the way everyone else does it, but they find a way to make things happen in their favor.
- Sometimes it's easier and more profitable to change the players than to change the game.
- You do not always need all the facts or eyes on the investment to make the right decisions. In order to win, bet on winners. In most transactions, you are betting primarily on people. Follow your gut feelings.
- Don't be afraid to give, or get, tough advice.
- Ask and you shall receive.
- No one says yes to a request you do not make.
- If you're not getting a lot of noes, you're missing a lot of yesses.
- Entrepreneurs have to be ready for opportunity. Sometimes it doesn't knock twice.
- Use no as the starting point, not as the finish line.

- Don't rush into accepting investor money and get locked in to one investor. If you do something for the money now, you may regret it later on. Your ideal investors will bring more to the table than just money.
- Put your eggs in one basket.
- Know your stakeholders.
- Don't allow short-term benefits to be detrimental to your game-winning homerun. Be the biggest risk-taker in your deals.
- As you build your business, make sure that you—not a supplier or a customer—are in charge and in control your destiny.
- If you can see John Jones through John Jones's eyes, you can sell John Jones what John Jones buys.
- Do your research and understand what motivates someone.
- Mistakes are a part of life. Admit them, address them, and move on.
- Always look for the gems that hide in the rubble.
- Be specific with your plan. Many brilliant entrepreneurs have failed without a clear plan. It's awfully hard to get there if you don't know where you're going.
- Draw your own conclusions, and plan and negotiate accordingly.
- Don't predict. Protect.
- Dollars are only a small part of compensation.
- Value first—compensation second.
- Your time is valuable. Don't be afraid to disrupt an industry's current process in favor of a better one. This philosophy applies to every industry.
- Build a legacy and a business based on integrity.
- Selling a product or business doesn't have to be about addressing needs. People make decisions based on desire. Sell to what people want, and you'll always win.

- Make sure your business includes having fun.
- There's always a market for excellence and quality.
- You can't create a market. Opportunity lies in identifying and serving unserved and underserved markets.
- If you're going to jump in, do it with decisive action. My personal translation is, "Get big or get out."
- Choose your fights carefully. Are they really worth the time, effort, and expense?
- If you maintain your ethics and integrity, you can disagree on business issues without destroying personal relationships.
- If you deal with a skunk long enough, you are bound to get sprayed.
- Define your market on the front end, and don't lose money trying to be all things to all people.
- Get it right. Choose a tagline and logo that is simple, memorable, and descriptive.
- Do your due diligence, do your research, and be aware of what's out there.
- Taking time to contact the debtor and asking if they would like you to buy their note totally changes the relationship and dynamics.
- Leverage your loyalty.
- When you're recruiting for your company, seize the moment: "Cut a walking stick when you find it."
- Understand the tax laws and understand your rights. You can live a good deal longer and/or better on the same income if Uncle Sam isn't sharing a big paycheck with you.
- Don't let "big" overshadow "profitable."
- Every new technology or advancement isn't necessarily a good deal for you or your business.

- Success often eludes the one-trick pony. Look for more tricks or another buyer.
- Timing is critical when soliciting donations for worthy causes.
- If you're an entrepreneur, it's inevitable that you'll eventually be the only one who believes in a decision you've got to make. Go against the grain. Take risks. Bet on yourself.

— Acknowledgments —

It is with a great deal of pride that I recognize the personal assistance and support I received from four of the world's top entrepreneurial leaders/teachers. Listed alphabetically: Norm Brodsky, Verne Harnish, Carrie Santos, Gino Wickman.

A loving thanks and a pearl necklace to my wife, Bettye. She has been at my side in several of my ventures and has provided many of the less glorious elements of sweat, tears, and long hours required for the successful execution of those visions.

The board of directors are the key forces behind our nonprofit 501(c)(3), Biz Owners Ed, and they all deserve my thanks and appreciation, not only for this book but for the major roles they play in changing hundreds of entrepreneurial lives for the better, creating thousands of jobs and, in doing so, strengthening the foundation of our great country. The board: Bill Brown, Bruce Brown, Dave Casey, Rick Garrett, Wayne Gono, David Hammer, Bettye Rodgers, and other key players: Tony Hartl, Rick Hopper, Joe Kesterson, Rick Sapio, Zane Tarence, Jason Williford, Jeff York. Thank you to my current and prior personal assistants, Maribel Morales and Jessica Crawford, for their constant support and encouragement during the writing of this book.

A very special thank you to two very special people. David W. Hammer—my very dear friend and my M&A attorney who has handled the sale of my last fourteen companies, and the man who insisted that I start committing my entrepreneurial experiences to paper. As I told my tales, he actually typed the first draft of many of the stories in this book as we cruised across the Atlantic Ocean on holiday. As to the second individual, remember I told you my bet was one that I could not lose. Because of THE BET, the publisher provided me with the world's best coach, guiding light, collaborator, and sounding board, Bonnie Hearn Hill.

I always tell my mentees that the single most important action in their life and career is surrounding themselves with great people. I truly believe God has guided me in my personal effort to do so. Among those not named above that hold, in my entrepreneurial and small business world, top spots on a very very long list: Frank Adams, Jim Attrell, Mike Brown, Krish Dhanam, Don Dykstra, Tony Jeary, Doug Renfro, Fergus Reynolds, Tim Shiner, Johnelle van Eeden, Steven Van Ooyen.

— About the Author —

Jay D. Rodgers is *the* entrepreneur's mentor. He has founded and sold numerous successful ventures including Smart Start, now the nation and the world's largest breath-alcohol, ignition-interlock company. Rodgers was the visionary for and cofounder of Biz Owners Ed, a nonprofit organization that provides an entrepreneurial program and community for business owners seeking knowledge, advice, and tools to take the next leap forward in their businesses. He and his wife, Bettye, have homes in Fort Worth and Flower Mound, Texas, where he mentors small-business owners. Visit his website: www.JayRodgersAuthor.com.